TAROT MINORS

G.O.M.

Know all the Elements
Reveal through Nature;
Show how that Minor Key
Could not be Greater.

Tarot Minors
G.O.M.
(Grigory Ottonovich von Mebes)

English Translation of text, copyright © 2020 Shin Publications
First Edition

Published 2020 by Shin Publications, England
All rights reserved

ISBN: 978-1-9163365-1-3

http://alchemical-weddings.com/

Dedicated to Our Lady of all Nations
and St Bartholomew

Holy Father, Holy Son, Holy Spirit

Fig. 39.

Holy Mother, Holy Daughter, Holy Soul

CONTENTS

About the Author

The collegiate adviser Baron Gregory Ottonovich Mebes (G.O.M.) was born in Riga in 1868. After graduating in 1891 from the Physics and Mathematics Faculty of St. Petersburg University, he gave up his career and devoted himself entirely to the study of "secret knowledge".

In the 1904-1905 school year he taught physics and mathematics at the Czarskoye Selo real school and the Nikolaev gymnasium, as well as physics at the women's school of the Ministry of Public Education; in 1906-1917 he taught mathematics in the Page Corps and Nikolaevsk Cadet Corps. His first wife was Olga Yevgrafovna Nagornova, with whom he broke in 1912, which did not prevent her from subsequently playing a prominent role in Martinism.

The Martinist Lodge, which was a branch of the French Order of the same name (the Kabbalistic Order of the Rose and the Cross), was founded in Russia by the French occultist Gerard Encausse, known under the pseudonym Papus. At the end of 1910, Mebes became the Inspector General (Secretary) of the St. Petersburg branch of the Order, and in 1911-1912 he read in St. Petersburg a lecture course on the Encyclopedia of the Occult, which followed Papus' theory in almost everything. These lectures, published under the pseudonym of G.O.M., were very popular, as evidenced by dozens of memories and reviews.

In August 1912, Mebes tried to be free from the tutelage of the Paris leaders, announcing the proclamation of the independence of the Russian Martinists. The Apollonia lodge, headed by Mebes, (with the initiatory name of Butator[1]) was declared a great lodge (Grand Council of Russia). The situation was cleared up by the end of 1912, after the official report by Mebes, Papus's report

---

[1] Guardian Angel Butator is the regent of calculations, who serves in the third hour of the day and is invoked during ritual magic.

about his break with him and the establishment in Russia of an independent order called "Autonomous discharge of Martinism of Russian obedience" led by the "Invisible Master".

In 1913, St. Petersburg Martinists, led by Mebes, formed a special autonomous chain of O.M.O.R. with a pronounced Templar colour. In 1916, it was transformed into the "Order of Martinist Eastern Obedience". It was ruled by the Order of the "Invisible Master" or the Father (G.O.M.). His official representative was the student of Mebes, Inspector-General I.K. Antoshevsky (the initiatory name Hyacinthus). In the summer of 1917, when I.K. Antoshevsky was killed, he was replaced in this position by another student of G.O.M. – V.V. Bogdanov. The Chapter of the Order consisted of seven persons and the official print organ of the Russian Martinists was the occult magazine, Isis.

In 1918-1921 Mebes gave lectures on the Book of Zohar in Petrograd, and his second wife Maria Nesterova lectured on the history of religion. The declarative goal that the Russian Martinists had set for themselves was, on the one hand, to prepare the one going for the Highest Initiation (maximum programme), and on the other, to expand the esoteric secondary education of those who were not recognised as capable of the Highest Initiation. In addition to purely theoretical studies, practical work was carried out in the "school" to develop its capabilities for telepathy and psychometry among its members.

Aleksandr M Aseev[2], the publisher of the book "Occultism and Yoga", owns the version according to which all three main branches of the Russian initiating

---

[2] Aleksandr M. Aseev (1902-1993) was a medical doctor who, fascinated by Agni Yoga, struck up a correspondence with Nicholas Roerich in 1931 and went onto launch the publication, Occultism and Yoga, in Belgrade, guided by Helene Roerich, wife of Nicholas. The published correspondence between Aseev and Roerich was the highlight of the journal.

movement – Freemasonry, Martinism and Rosicrucianism – existed in the form of separate and independent organisations. However, they were led by the same person – G.O. Mebes. Needless to say, all three orders worked in close contact with each other and often included the same persons. Martinist and Rosicrucian lodges were located, according to A.M. Aseev, in the apartment of Mebes in the Sands and were beautifully furnished. The text commentator on A.M. Aseev, N. A. Bogomolov, notes, however, that in fact, Mebes' apartment was not in Sand, but at the corner of Greek Avenue and 5th Rozhdestvenskaya Street. This is in fact the case, but Bogomolov does not take into account the fact that in 1917 – early 1918, Mebes really lived for some time in Peski, where he was a teacher. All this indicates that A.M. Aseev was very, very well informed, and his information can, therefore, be trusted, although his conclusion that Mebes was supposedly the unofficial leader of the initiating movement in Russia, not only at the beginning of the century, but also in the 1920s, is a clear exaggeration. Another thing is that the Masons, the Martinists, and the Rosicrucians, in essence, are links of one chain – they have always worked and work in close contact with each other. Their secretive activity in Russia, and then in the USSR, continued until 1925, when the OGPU became seriously interested in their groups and work. In the middle of 1928, the Leningradskaya Pravda and Krasnaya Zvezda newspapers reported that "an investigation into the Great Lodge Astraea, led by 70-year-old Black Occultist Mebes, was opened by KGB agents". The investigation, as claimed by the newspaper, soon showed that Leningrad had "quite serious Masonic lodges with several dozen members, with Masters, with dedication, oaths signed by blood, statute, foreign correspondence and membership fees."
According to AM Aseev, Grigori Ottonovich Mebes died in Ust-Sysolsk in 1930.

Nicolay Georgevich Rogalev Girs

Nabusar[3]

*"Today again unfurled the ancient flag of the order
preserved in our hearts and we inclined our heads before
the luminous memory of our teachers and brothers to
continue serving the great work of truth, beauty and
goodness"*

Nicolas Georgevich Rogalev Girs was born in Czarist
Russia on June 15 1898 and joined the
military school of St Petersburg at age 14. He came
under the spiritual tutelage of G.O.M., receiving, at the
age of 21, the Martinist initiation within the Nordic Star
Order on December 20 1919.

As was the case with fellow student, Nina Rudnikoff,
Girs escaped the Red Terror of the Bolshevik Revolution,
although it is unknown if they left Russia together.
Whilst Nina gave her notes from the G.O.M. course to
Catarina Sreznewska-Zelenzeff, who took them to Brazil,
Girs went with some students to Germany where he
continued the work.

Having survived the Bolsheviks, he would go on to
experience the similarly egregious advancement of
Hitler, who put a stop to the initiatory schools and
persecuted occultists. Whilst Gris himself managed to
survive both terrors, he decided to leave Germany for
Chile on August 14, 1948, with a view to dedicating his

---

[3] We are unsure regarding the precise origin and meaning of this
mystery name but note that in ancient Mesopotamia there was
Nabu, patron god of literacy, vegetation, the rational arts, scribes
and wisdom. There can also be found ancient Assyrian inscriptions
which refer to one, Nabu-sar-usur, who may have been the royal cup
bearer.

life to painting and the restoration of art works in Santiago.

It was during this time in Santiago that Girs encountered a group of Martinists who'd kept the flame of the tradition alive. A new Martinist movement was thus born in Chile and by 1957 there were several orders across the country, one of which had a direct connection with the Paris Order led by Philippe Encause, son of Papus, from whom were received new rituals and administrative rules. Girs was nominated as the great national delegate for Chile and tasked with forming a major council.

Girs was known to engage in very profound and intense spiritual work and by 1960 had done much to advance Martinism in Chile. In addition to his affiliation to Martinism, for half a century he was also a member of the sovereign sanctuary of The Ancient and Primitive Rite of Memphis and Misraim. Thus he represented, in his own Grand Lodge, the latest initiate in the uninterrupted chain of Russian Martinists and Freemasons founded in Moscow in 1788, directly linked to Louis Claude Saint-Martin himself through Prince Alexey Golizin.

The "Occult Encyclopedia" of G.O.M. – published in English as the Tarot Majors Course – was Girs' primary initiatory study material. Through his contact with other Russian initiates living in Central America he also obtained the notes of the Minor Arcana which were used to configure the South American Autonomous Martinist Grand Lodge.

Nicolay Rogalev Girs passed away on December 12 1979 and was buried in the Russian cemetery at Puente Alto.

The Minor Arcana of the Tarot

According to the teachings of G.O.M.

In world literature, presentations of the Minor Arcana are rare, not as a method of divination, but as a vehicle for the ascension of man towards the highest spiritual achievements.

This one path of constant internal effort – the path of Ethical Hermeticism - includes many degrees. However, for clarity, it was divided into four main stages: **Coins, Swords, Cups** and **Wands**.

In the present book, the first two steps - especially the degrees of Coins - are presented in more detail, as they are understandable to every human being in whom the aspiration has manifested to the highest level.

For this reason, the last two stages of the Cups and, even more so, of Wands, will seem less complete. This is inevitable, because the level of these steps is so far above that of the vast majority of human beings, that the experiences would not be understandable to them.

It would be useless to talk to a boy who is attending the first degree of teaching on the formulas of modern physics. The maximum that could be achieved would be a general and vague idea of the attainment.

The human being at the foot of the stairs whose top is far above in the clouds does not see the higher degrees. However, as the various steps are being reached, the view of the lower levels of the heights becomes increasingly clear. Likewise, as the human being rises spiritually, the experiences of World Cups and Wands are becoming more understandable and, what the words of a book could not explain, becomes an internal Truth that is acquired.

Some knowledge of Kabbalah and esoteric meaning of the Major Arcana would better illustrate the internal states presented in this book. If there is no difficulty derived from studying these subjects, reading can be continued without paying attention to references to the

Major Arcana or the Sephiroth. The book will still be comprehensible, because it describes the path that the soul must go through to reach perfection. This one is the target that, regardless of the method chosen, remains the same for everyone. People who would like to follow the passage of the soul through the Sephiroth can use the diagram here.

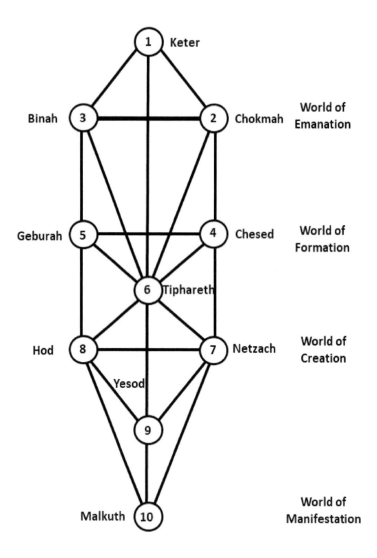

According to tradition, when the Egyptian priests, heirs of Atlantic Wisdom, were still guardians of Sacred Mysteries, the Great Hierophant, predicting a time of spiritual decay of humanity and the persecution of sacred teaching, called to the temple all wise priests of Egypt so that together they could find a means of preserving initiation teachings from destruction, thus allowing their application to generate the distant future. Many suggestions were made, but the wisest among those present said that due to the moral decline of humanity, addiction prevailed everywhere, so it was suggested that Eternal Truths should be preserved and perpetuated through addiction, until the time when, again, they could be taught.

So it was done and the great symbolic system of Esoteric Wisdom - the Tarot - was given to humanity in the form of a deck of 78 cards, which for thousands of years served to satisfy human curiosity about the future or served as a distraction where people killed time by playing games.

In these 78 cards - 22 "Major Arcana" and 56 "Minor Arcana - the Egyptian wise men encoded all wisdom they had inherited, all the knowledge they had, all the Truth that was accessible to them about God, the Universe and Man. The fixed structure of the system prevented any misrepresentation and Tarot, even today, remains a source of wisdom for those with eyes to see and ears to hear its silent language.

According to Tradition, only after studying and understanding the 22 Major Arcana and their cards, could the disciple then study the Minor Arcana, as they are deeper and more abstract and, due to their metaphysical nature, cannot be represented by images and allegories, like the Major Arcana. Their understanding was conditioned by the disciple's evolutionary level.

About the Major Arcana there is a wide range of information in world literature. They are also represented in numerous works of art from past centuries. Various thinkers, philosophers and occultists such as Jean-Baptiste Alliette (Etteilla), Stanislas de Guaita, Eliphas Levi, Papus, Oswald Wirth and others, studied and wrote about them.

It is interesting to verify that some authors wrote about the Major Arcana without ever mentioning them, so that an entire book can be read without the reader suspecting that it is about the Arcana. Such works are, for example: Dogme et Rituel de la Haute Magie by Eliphas Levi; Tableau Naturel des Rapports by Louis Claude de Saint Martin and others. The reason why the authors acted in this way was probably to protect the underlying esoteric source.

With regard to the Minor Arcana, outside the manuals of taromancy, we are not aware that there is any literature about this grand scheme of the path, which represent the first steps of the disciple to the highest achievements and reintegration. In the Russian language, we find just a short explanation about the Minor Arcana in the "Course of Encyclopaedia of the Occult" (Tarot Majors Course) by G.O.M.

Until now, the Minor Arcana were studied only in closed circles of initiation schools, This, to avoid perhaps that knowledge would fall into the hands of those looking not for the real "Way", but the paths for personal aggrandisement. At the present time, however, the Spiritual Light is no longer to be hidden. The awakening of souls is necessary. Those who have not yet matured enough for the absorption of certain truths will pass without realising them. For others, however, knowing how to find out for themselves the dangerous points that such knowledge contains would necessitate a deep study of esotericism which, in itself, would result in an internal sublimation.

In the Middle Ages there were several alchemists who started the work wanting to get rich and they ended up being wise and immune to earthly temptations.

The truths, the deeper and higher they go, the less there is that can be explained to others or understood intellectually. You need your own, internal experience to be able to capture them. Esoteric knowledge can never be transmitted in its entirety, neither orally nor in writing. Meditation, internal experience and intuition are indispensable. Then, little by little, it becomes wisdom. It is also impossible to explain the Truth in accurate terms; only approaches can be used. The truth, by its nature, it is inexpressible and cannot be limited by any means. We can even say that each word, in a sense, is a lie, because the spirit of the word is not transmissible. Only symbols allow us to get rid of that limitation.

A symbol is not just a symbol but a means of intellectual apprehension; it is also a starting point for tuition. The symbol, in addition to being understood must be felt. Meditation on the symbol, its image, its internal sense, leads to something much deeper than intellectual understanding.

The Minor Arcana system is symbolised by a deck of 56 cards, divided into four suits: Coins (Coins), Swords (Swords), Cups (Cups) and Wands (Wands). Each suit has 10 numeric cards of 1 to 10 and 4 figures: the king, the lady, the knight and the jack (in the modern deck, the Knights have been deleted). The structure of the Minor Arcana obeys two numerical systems: the fourth and the decimal. The 4 suits correspond to the four main stages of human development:

Coins: The stage of external and internal acquisitions of personality in terrestrial life:

Swords: The devaluation of these acquisitions, the internal fight, the negation of the world and the personality itself;

Cups: Uniting with the Divine Will;

Wands: Power and fulfilment.

On the edge of the 1st Major Arcana, these four stages are symbolised by four "tools of the Wizard". The quaternary law, expressed in the form of 4 suits, is repeated, within the limits of each suit, by the 4 figures of this suit.

The entire system of the Arcana - Major and Minor - is closely connected with the Mystical Kabbalah of Judaism, the Sephirothic system and the sacred Tetragrammaton or divine name Iod-He-Vau-He (יהוה). This is not surprising, if we consider that it is believed that Moses, the creator of the kabbalistic system, was an initiate of the Egyptian temples.

It can be said that the Sephirothic Tree, with its extension through the four worlds, wherein there is everything that exists, is a deeply symbolic arrangement of the Arcana system. The 4 suits and 4 figures of the Minor Arcana correspond to these 4 worlds of the Sephirotic Tree. The letters numerically correspond to the 10 Sephiroth. In addition, these cards are linked to the first 10 Major Arcana and, through their particular number (or the sum of digits of this number), with a Major Arcanum of the second or third decade.

If the quaternary division of the Minor Arcana indicates the stages that each soul in search of the Light must go through, the decimal debt - in this case the 10 numerical letters - indicates how it should go through them.

The 22 paths of the Sephirothic Tree (the links between the Sephiroth) correspond to the Major Arcana and are the many keys to understanding of the Sephiroth and, therefore, of the Minor Arcana. Each of these channels - and several channels can lead to a Sefira - adds esoteric aspects to the basic meaning determined by the Sefira, thus facilitating its understanding. The study of Kabbalah. of the Major Arcana is very useful in helping us to understand the Minor Arcana.

The 4 suits, starting with the highest - Wands - present a succession of the active and passive stages that correspond to the succession of the active and passive principles of the Tetragrammaton. The relationship between the elements Iod-He-Vau-He (יהוה), the court cards and suits of the Minor Arcana, the Sephirotic worlds and the realisations of human spiritualities, can be tabulated as follows:

IHVH	SUITS	FIGURES	SEPHIROTHIC WORLD	INITIATION CORRESPONDENCE
IOD	WANDS	KINGS	EMANATION	3rd & 4th Initiation
HE	CUPS	QUEENS	CREATION	
VAU	SWORDS	KNIGHTS	FORMATOIN	2nd Initiation
SECOND HE	COINS	JACKS	MANIFESTATION	1st Initiation

We see through this scheme that initiatic progress, since Coins to Wands, follow the opposite direction of the Tetragrammaton letters, because it starts at the second He and gradually rises to Iod. This is logical because it is not [an aspect of] the law of Creation (descent), but of the path of spiritual reintegration, which is a process of sublimation and passage of the dense to the subtle, until the soul returns to its Primordial Source.

The two opposite directions of passing through the Arcana are traditionally called "diabetic" – the descent - and "anabatic" - the ascent. The diabetic way leads from the subtle to the dense; anabatic from the dense to the subtle.

The first is critical, that is, it corresponds to manifest to that of the higher principles at the lower levels. The second is a process of sublimation. The first, in the scheme of the Minor Arcana, corresponds to Hermetic Philosophy, that is, by unveiling the Laws of the Universe; the second corresponds to Ethical

Hermeticism, that is, when rising on the evolutionary scale through the sublimation of the lower nature.

Both processes are possible, both in the entire system of the 4 suits, as well as within the limits of each one. Depending on the case and human individuality, this or that direction is more appropriate.

The figures of the Minor Arcana are, first of all, symbols of the 4 suits. Each of the 4 figures of each suit concentrates the characteristics of one of the 4 suits, besides the suit to which he or she belongs. Thus, the Kings corresponds to the suit of Wands, Queens to the Suit of Cups, Knights to the Swords and Jacks to the Coins. Being thus, the King of Wands, for example, will represent a double influence of Wands and will often be called "Wand of Wands "; the Queen of Cups:" Cup of Cups ", etc. Each one of these letters, together with all the numerical letters of their own suit, represents the pure essence of that suit (for example, the Queen of Cups with 10 numerical cards of Cups or the Knight of Swords together with 10 numerical Spade cards).

Out of these basic divisions and "pure" influences of a single suit, there is, of course, a multitude of influences composed, which express unique human individuality, its specific, unrepeatable tonality. This "unique hue" can be conserved even in the very high stages on the spiritual path. The experience of each suit can be lived under one or more additional influences from other suits. Thus, the experience, for example, of Coins, lived under the influence of Cups or Wands, will characterise the most spiritually elevated of that experience. The experience of Swords, lived under the influence of Coins, will define the less mystical way to cross the stage of Swords. However, between crossing Swords under the additional influence of Coins and crossing Coins under the influence of Swords, there will be a very big difference.

Each suit has, it could be said, a dominant idea. These ideas are:

Coins: Establish support points in the plans to reach a "starting point" of suspension", that is, a contact with the superior planes;

Swords: free yourself from the illusions of the lower worlds and reach a new spiritual birth;

Cups: raise the lower, transmitting it, through sacrifice, to what was received from above;

Wands: be aware of your mission in the scheme of the Divine Plan for Earth and work accordingly, in contact with your Higher self.

The figures of a suit, within the limits of that suit, represent the four initiatory levels, at which unfold the experience of a particular suit. In this way, the Minor Arcana have 64 basic internal stages of the disciple's spiritual path, that is, the experiences of the 4 suits in their 4 aspects and 4 levels, which corresponds to the formula 4 x 4 x 4 = 64 which, by the sum of the figures, leads to the final individuality.

The study of the Minor Arcana can be done under completely different aspects, such as: Taromancy, Astrology, Alchemy, Ethical Hermetism, Philosophy, Hermetic Philosophy, Christian Esoterism, Pure Mystique, Magic, Kabbalah, etc.

We think that for some students of these aspects, such as the Ethical Hermeticism or path of spiritual evolution, the Minor Arcana offer more possibilities for a clear and detailed study, especially in their higher stages, than the Major Arcana. These, however, although they encompass all evolutionary and involutive manifestations of life, mainly deal with the path of Coins and the magical initiation (especially the first 10 and 4 last Arcana).

From what has just been said, it can be deduced that the Arcana content cannot be exhausted by a written or oral presentation, however good it may be. Only the fields belonging to these Arcana be outlined and understood by those who are rich in ideas, esoteric truths or scientific knowledge, hidden knowledge and individual reactions. Arcana, by the same token, cannot be taught. You can only be on the path that leads to your understanding.

Each deep meditation on an Arcana allows us to glimpse ever-new facets of Truth. In the Arcana system, even the smallest details are symbolic; the signs of the suits, the number and the way of grouping, the figure they form, everything has an esoteric sign and all these are key details for some aspect of knowledge. The progress of each new stage is, of course, conditioned by the level of internal realisation of the previous step.

An experience (or cycle of experiences) which has not been exhausted, will be restarted again, usually at a level and keeping the same individual tone. A human being, always going deeper into the experience of a suit, can reach, through that suit, to the highest mystical states.

This Tarot Minors course presents what could be called "a general picture "of passing through the suits and their degrees, because it will not take into account the characteristics of individual disciples, nor the appropriate methods to address them individually. If the disciple has the privilege of having an instructor, he will know how to guide them individually. In the absence of the instructor, serious literature could help you in your work. This is the purpose of the gift of this course.

In relation to the complete path of the four suits, we will follow the anabatic direction, that is, we will start with Coins, raising ourselves to Wands, because in this method certain internal processes present themselves in a more understandable way. We will present the path of each suit at its highest level, that is, from the wands and in its own aspect, to determine, "Swords of Swords", "Cups of Cups ", etc., limiting the more general manifestations. We have expanded only upon the stage of Coins, then show how the higher degrees of Coins, enter the experience of the highest suits. Someone, performing the stage of Coins in its total extension and depth, would reach the highest evolutionary states, up until the very Mission of the Hierophant of Wands.

In our presentation of the Arcana, we will use the deductive method, that is, we will start with the central idea of the Arcana, seeking to develop and illustrate it. Before moving on to the detailed study of each of the 10 initial degrees of the Coins suit, we will make a brief outline of each suit.

COINS

The Coins stage corresponds to transformation of the common matter of human personality into a more subtle and tightened substance. This terror called the initiation process and its progress depends on two factors: the disciple's personal scourge and the penetration of Spiritual Light. Dread will always be necessary; as for Light, it can better penetrate the disciple as your spiritual level rises and the more you raise the level of the disciple's spiritual life, the greater his thirst for Light, until

You let him devote all his torments to the search for that Light.

Coins, in addition to the traditional graphic symbol (fig. 1), also has an esoteric symbol: two adjacent cups horizontally crossed by a wand and, vertically, by a sword (fig. 2).

This symbol means that Coins contains within itself, potentially, the three other suits and that the highest human achievements can be achieved through the physical plane.

The evolutionary stage of Coins, that is, that of the second He, the densest element of the name Iod-He-Vau-He (יהוה) corresponds to the level of a man whose feet are firmly in the physical plane, who has well-founded ideas, convictions and opinions, that values the personal "I" and everything that the same achieves or acquires. At the Coins level, there are several types of realisation on the astral plane. It also belongs to alchemy which is an analogy of Ethical Hermetism, that is, of the transmutation of personality.

The most typical expression of an initiate of Coins is a white magician who has developed all the internal and external gifts of his personality and has full dominion both over himself and over the astral plane.

At the Coins stage, the disciple's progress is usually directed by a master, be he incarnate or disincarnated. At this stage there are many types and degrees of initiation. They are usually rites of different Orders and Fraternities or, then, of massive branches. Most are purely external ceremonies, without any correlation with the internal state of the initiate.

In reality, in the Coins stage there are 4 basic degrees of Beginnings that, in the ascending order, correspond respectively to the levels of the Jack, the Knight, the Queen and the King. The beginning of the Jack rank covers only the physical plane and usually results from a contact that initiates established with some spiritual egregore, or, their decision to dedicate themselves to a job, either for their own spiritual evolution or for the evolution of the environment where they are. This is the first step on the initiatic path

The next initiate, that of Knights, corresponds to the magical, astral initiation linked to the Shin mystery (see the 21st Major Arcanum) and grants the initiate dominion over certain astral entities and manifestations. This initiation includes the opening of certain psychic centres, without any such domain being possible.

The beginnings of the third and fourth degrees - that of the Queen and that of the King of Coins is, in its essence, just a beginning having two different aspects, depending on the predominance, at the beginning, of

the male or female element, or that is, one's gender.
This entails a certain difference at the beginning.
One of the important achievements of the Coins
internship is, as we will see later, the approximation of
the androgynous state, both in the sense of developing
within the self the principles of the two polarities and,
later, to approach the realisation of the external,
spiritual androgyne.
The beginnings of the third and fourth degrees are
initiated Hermetically. They correspond to the mental
plane and grant the initiated a certain power over their
thoughts and greater spiritual insight.
However, simultaneously with all the achievements and
internal and external successes, the world is losing its
value for a disciple and initiate of Coins. He finds out
that everything he accomplished with so much scorch is
nothing but an illusion. I enter, naked inside, like a
newborn child, start looking for the REAL. This is the
ticket to the next suit: Swords.

SWORDS

There are several symbols of this suit. The
traditional presents the union of the two
symbols of the upper suits: The Cups and the
Wands which, together, form the figure of
Lingam. The esoteric symbol is a sword, the tip
of which is directed upwards. Its , in the form of
the cross with equal arms, that is, the cross of
the 4 elements, indicates the elementary
composition of the human being. A channel
runs through the card of the sword from the to
the tip, symbolising the union with the world of
Logos.
In the Swords stage, the spiritual pilgrim no more has a
master, not even anyone who could point the way. for
him, it is a period of complete solitude. Internal growth

is no longer encouraged by ceremonies or rituals. This stage also consists of 4 degrees, but these are purely esoteric and perceptible only to observers from the upper planes. The disciple himself knows nothing of his/her progress. The Swords stage can be crossed in two ways:

a) on the path of faith, positive, aspiring and seeking serve the Logos in His redemptive work and
b) in the negative way, sometimes called "way of the strong", way of rebellion against the Logos and the state of the world. In this, the human being crosses the whole Sephirothic Tree, that is, the 10 degrees of the suit, fighting and isolating itself from the creative aspects of each Sefira. Rebellion against the external world (Malkuthh), rejects the form (Yesod), negates the value of power and peace (Netzach and Hod), denies the possibility of harmony (Tiphereth), denies mercy and Justice (Gedulah and Geburah), reason and wisdom (Binah and Chokmah), arriving at denial of life (Keter). These sufferings and the internal emptiness they lead to, reaching its peak, awaken in the pilgrim an immense thirst and need to satiate it with something perfect and totally pure: The passage to the World Cup suit.
With regard to the next two stages – Cups and Wands - very little can be said, because the more the internal level rises, so much less can it be expressed by words.

CUPS

The Cups stage corresponds to the first He of the word IHVH (יהוה), the passive and receptive He. The traditional and esoteric symbol of Cups it is a chalice, always filled with the Divine Light. It cannot be empty.
There is no more affirmation of personality (Coins) and individuality (Swords). The sufferings disappear, burned

in their own fuel. The place of self-conscience is taken by the conscience of the Divine. The experience of the Eternal is being lived. The existence resembles the waves of the ocean, yet is intensely real. The spirit joins the Logos. It is no more living man; Christ lives within the man.

WANDS

The fourth and last stage corresponds to the word IHVH: the active ingredient. However, Wands are unimaginable without Cups and Cups inseparable from Wands. Here there is not only passivity or just activity, because one of the stages is passive-active and the other active-passive. In Wands, as in Cups, there are not and cannot be external graduations. Everything is internal.

The traditional symbol of Wands is a trunk of tree with 4 pruned branches (fig. 6); is the manifestation of the Law of Iod-He-Vau-He (יהוה).

Wands represent the highest human achievement. At this stage, the man, always receptive to the radiations of the Divine Light collaborates consciously with the Divine plan on the Earth. It transmits to others the Light that he now possesses in abundance and that, in spite of being divided, never diminishes

The last grades of a suit participate in the experience of the next suit. In this way, the last card of Swords is integrated into the Cups. The last two Cups will join the Wands. In the case of Wands, the last three cards represent the three different portal that lead to the Fountain of Light.

20

COINS

The Coins suit is the suit of human personality and its basic objective is the internal organisation, purification and multilateral development of that personality, taking in time the expansion of consciousness, growth of the realising power and the formation of individuality.
The purposes of a Coins student are personal achievements, both internal and external, including the material plane. At this stage, the human will still remains personal, although it is already starting to become evolutionary.
The work of a Student - as in all other suits - goes through ten stages, which correspond to the fields of influence of the ten Sephiroth. These steps, however, are not fixed or equal for all. If the lesson of a stage has not been sufficiently learned, the disciple will have to return to it, perhaps even several times, going through it a little differently each time and generally within a higher level. At the same time, the other Sephiroth will continue to exercise their influence and exert additional impact on the student's life and work.
In this course we will present the outline of a basic path, straight and ideal, in which the lessons of each stage are learned entirely, without the need to return to them. We will present these to you, as already said, at their higher spiritual level and in the greatest amplitude. In real life, this 'model way' almost doesn't exist. The level is rarely so high, the experience is more broad and the path is not always straight. Failures and deviations from the straight path are numerous.
The development of the psycho-physical constitution of the being and the appearance of occult powers, until then latent, are, in general, consequences of a conscious work in that direction and certain exercises that, for the most part, have a purely hidden character, and that the disciple of Coins began to practice.

Because of this, the suit of Coins is sometimes called "hidden suits".

It is important to underline that these exercises always aim for the development of forces belonging to several subplanes of the astral world. As for the spiritual principle, this cannot be developed by exercises, but the same, along with a self-imposed discipline, that is, imposed by evolving will, result in a general subtlety that it can facilitate the handling of the spirit. In the highest plane there will be no exercise. The process will be fully internal.

At the end of the book are added several exercises, including practical supplements for each degree of Coins. We do remember, however, that in the path of Ethical Hermeticism the essential factor is the sincere search for Spiritual Light and not some advantages achieved by exercises.

The Coins path can also be covered by different routes, for example, following one of the established religions, its disciplinary methods and rituals. The person then attaches himself to the particular egregore of that religion, which will play an important role in his/her life.

On the path of the occult, the choice of the egregore – in the case that it actually exists - the spiritual master and the working method belong to the student.

Orthodox ways are generally limited to moral discipline; occultism, moreover, aims at the development of latent psychic powers. However, the main difference between the two paths is that the orthodox is based on faith and occultism on knowledge. In the first, the development of feeling is sought, in the second, of reason. Therefore, when, in the first, the person is ready to pass to the stage of Swords, in the majority of cases, it will move towards the positive aspect of this suit; in the second, towards its negative or philosophical aspect.

At the Coins stage, during the first seven degrees, the personality becomes tight and gradually subtle. The realisation of the eighth grade allows the disciple to attain identification of their individuality. The ninth grade represents the esoteric beginning of this suit, that is, the creative synthesis of everything that was reached on the way to Coins. The tenth grade corresponds to the manifestation of this synthesis in the world of "non-I". The first seven Arcana (or degrees) are under the influence of the Seven Secondary Causes; the last three - under the three Primordial Causes.

The Coins stage covers everything that belongs to the occult and that, sufficiently accomplished, transforms a common man into a perfect white wizard. This transformation of personality finds its analogy in alchemical transmutation and each alchemical stage is correlated to one numerical chart of Coins. Alchemy, as a hidden science, corresponds, on the physical plane, to the initiation process of the soul. The basic degrees of transmutation follow suit. The essential difference is that, in the case of alchemy, the "impulse from Above" which transmutes the material elements in the "philosophical stone" comes from the initiated alchemist himself.

ACE OF COINS

Correspondence: SEFIRA KETER
Major Arcana 1, 10 and 19

The "1" always expresses the idea of some totality

Given the esoteric aspect, the "1" contains the starting point for the creative process (the beginning of deduction) and the return point for the unit (the beginning of induction).

Everything that exists, in all planes, is a reflection of the **ONE**; everything emanates from the Unity, and it returns to it.

These movements - the emanation and the return - are the basis of the esoteric teaching on the cyclical development of everything that evolves. This evolution accomplishes, through the multiple division of the primitive oneness, the successive return to a more perfect uniqueness and a new division and multiplication of the same.

The first Arcana of Coins begins, not just its own suit, but also the entire Minor Arcana system and potentially contains it in itself. It is the most abstract of all the Arcana and represents the IDEA that permits the acquisition of Coins, the profit and the suffering of the Swords, the bliss of Cups and the realisation of Wands. The Ace of Coins is also an analogue of the 1st Major Arcanum and, on the initiatic path, it corresponds to awareness; by the student that, in addition to all the manifestations and psycho-animics, there is something in it that is able to govern them and to evaluate them from an ethical point of view, of being "the voice of conscience". This something and the "Divina Esséncia" (the title of the 1st Major Arcana) that unites all the elements that compose it, making it a totality that is expressed for the first time initiatory formula of the way: **"I AM"**.

Due to all this, the subject of this Arcanum is so vast that in a general study like this, we have to limit ourselves to the main principles and, especially, the idea of oneness. The aspiration to uniqueness accompanies the entire path of Ethical Hermeticism. It is the reason why in the study of Ace of Coins we include a sketch of that path, in its most intense form, which is, the direct ascent by the central column of the Sephirotic Tree, with its four stages that form the basis of the entire initiatic process.

We start with the work that awaits the student who has just seen the initiatory path.

Be fully aware that everything that exists, in all planes, is a reflection of ONE. This awareness is indispensable for entering that path; however, the theoretical convictions, however high they may be, are not enough. The candidate for Initiation must be active, and his activity must begin within the self. It must realise its own uniqueness in all planes. How should the student prepare for this?

In his mind, the aspirant needs to determine for himself an objective that he can achieve in the distant future and remain firm in his decision and success. In the astral, you must use all your emotions to help to reach your chosen objective, in the physical plane to coordinate everything, so that your mental decision can be made.

In each one of his actions, the student must remain fully aware of what he is doing, what he wants and where he is going.

One of the biggest obstacles on the initiation path is the students' state of semi-awareness during most of their activities. This refers especially to daily actions, which are customarily executed without reflection, almost automatically. It is because of this semi-somnolence that some occult schools (those of Gurdjieff and Ouspensky, for example) require students to do exercises in order to develop a state of continuous consciousness, even in the most insignificant acts, in their reactions to the environment and even gestures. So, the student gets used to always being "awake" and responsible for their self, for their reactions, words and attitudes.

One of the recommendations made to students who are starting the Coins stage and that at first glance it might seem extraordinary, is not to let yourself get out of the chosen way, not even to do good works. In addition to involutive temptations, there are also evolutionary ones, and the student beginners should not be carried away by them. We do not want to suggest this means that good works are forbidden to him/her or that they must become selfish, but they must put everything aside which does not collaborate with the determined purpose. It should never depend on chance, the influence of others or the lack of self-control. However, and in any circumstances, the first duty of the aspirant is to fulfil their obligations.

Evidently, taking the initiatic path, the aspirant consciously rejected selfish pleasures and chose altruism, but this altruism must also be conscious and according to one's will, and not governed by emotions. It must be oriented and not dispersed by the circumstances.

Let us now move on to the question: how to achieve oneness in yourself.

The answer is given to us by the card of one of the Major Arcana, the 10th (The World). It shows us that it is necessary to rise above the murky waters of world chaos, climbing the Caduceus axis that supports the sphinx platform. This Caduceus is nothing other than a "stylisation" of the Sephirothic Tree.

Tradition teaches that in order to achieve final Oneness, the human being must "raise the axle", that is, rise up the column centre of the Sephirothic Tree.

The path of Coins, initiated by the feeling of Oneness (Sefira Keter) and leading the complete magical beginning, corresponds, within the limits of that suit, to a descent across all Sephiroth, gradually developing self-awareness and realising power.

However, the fact of feeling part of an ALL, this first glimpse of UNIFIED consciousness, is limited neither to the 1st Arcanum, nor to the Coins suit, but, traveling across all suits, it gets deeper and deeper, until the final Reintegration, because the target of every initiatic path, in all its degrees and stages, is the realisation of the union with the Divine. Thus, the path to Oneness, regardless of the symbolic sense in which the disciple approaches either suit, is always considered to be ASCENDANT.

In the Sephirothic Tree, the direct ascent to Oneness is symbolised by four central Sephiroth - Malkuth, Yesod, Tiphareth and Keter - and the channels that unite them: The 22 °, the 15 ° and the 3rd. This climb comprises four basic stages:

1. The dominance of the 22nd Arcanum, that is, the victory over the material world. In other words, the disciple must become internally independent of the constraints of the physical world.

2. Victory over the 15th Arcanum, that is, over all temptations, involutive tendencies and astral eddies, as well as the realisation of the domain over the forms of the astral world.

3. Liberation from mental illusions, realisation of harmony and a harmonious cosmo-vision, as well as the awareness that each particular life is a part of the One Life.

4. Realisation of what is symbolised, on the 10th Arcanum, through the platform of the sphinx. Crossing it, the human being passes to the Upper World, entering

into communion with the Divine. It's the last step on the way to the Oneness.

In order to follow this path of the Union, the disciple needs to reflect within themselves the four Aspects of God, called also "Divine Names" and corresponding to the four Sephiroth of the central column. Let's see this correspondence. at the ascending direction.

Sephira	Divine Name	Symbolic Principles
Malkuth	Adonai	Karma, Mercy, Justice
Yesod	El Chai / Shaddai	Miracles, Magic of Life and Death
Tiphareth	Eloah	Beauty and Harmony
Keter	Ehyeh	I am Me

To reflect the Adonai aspect, the disciple needs to "incarnate itself "its own karma, that is, understanding and accepting the full responsibility of your karma; one could say, merge with it, knowing that nothing happens by chance, that everything is interrelated and has its reason for being.
the second reflex - that of Shaddai - is to know how to let go, get away from everything that is unnecessary and that hinders spiritual progress. Develop in yourself the capacity for sacrifice, excluding, however, all and any element of emotion, The disciple must always be aware why and "in the name of" who he makes the sacrifice, what he "buys" with this sacrifice. So, according to expression of ancient wisdom, "that which benefits from the sacrifice incarnates in the person who sacrifices ".
In the life of the disciple, their will and their karma must be closely united; they need to be prepared and ready to accept karma in all its aspects, internal and external, positive and negative, good and bad. They need to consider their "happiness" as evidence of mercy,

sufferings as means of redemption and difficulties - as opportunities to exercise your willpower.

The third reflection - Eloah - Beauty and Harmony. Is called "Personality of the Cosmos" or "Ishvara", by Hindus. This corresponds to the awareness of permanent existence of your Higher Self, through all incarnations. Simultaneously with this awareness, the disciple must also be aware of the existence of the Higher Being of each of his fellow men. This will allow you to identify with others, to - say - "incarnate" in them, understand and feel them inside, even in the event of great difference in evolutionary level, character, etc. Such capacity comes from a deeper source than the simple understanding or sympathy. It is not just the basis of them, but much more.

The fourth reflex - Ehyeh - is the full awareness of being "born of the Spirit". This reveals the spiritual origin of everything that exists, the fact that everything is a coordinated network of causes and effects, having a higher purpose. The world is the temple of the Spirit. Evil comes from forgetfulness of that truth. Her understanding and realisation in life makes it possible to cross the "platform of the sphinx". Evidently, to get through it, a voluntary effort of will is indispensable, because this "platform" separates us from the "Kingdom of Heaven "of which it is necessary to seize by force.

In the field of art, as a symbolic example of such an aspiration of direct ascent through the central pillar of the Sephirothic Tree, is seen in the Gothic style of Medieval cathedrals, whose architecture, up to its smallest details, goes upwards. Let us remember that the builders of these cathedrals, who did not give us their names, but their ideas, were Freemasons.

The others two Major Arcana that correspond to the Ace of Coins are the 10th and 19th. The sum of both the numbers 10 and 19 is 1, which means that both are linked to the idea of Unity.

Let's move to the Major Arcana 19 °, trying to find supplementary information. Its hieroglyph is an axe.

With this axe, symbolizing the domain of the Arcanum 19 °, the disciple can open a breach and pass through the card platform of the 10 ° Arcanum. The sphinx, with respect to Coins, can be considered as the very essence of the Initiation or "Isis", and the platform that separates her from the disciple, like the "veils of Isis", or that is, the totality of imperfections which hide the Truth to the eyes of the disciple.

The card of Arcanum 19 has sun rays which, touching lands, they become Coins. It is the symbol of Ethical Hermeticism, of Spiritual Alchemy. In alchemy, the Ace de Coins corresponds to understanding that there is only one Primordial Substance, from which any transmutation is possible.

2 OF COINS

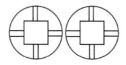

Correspondence: SEFIRA CHOKMAH
Major Arcana: 2, 11 and 20

The 1st Arcanum corresponds to the awareness of internal humidity; the 2nd to the awareness and harmonisation of internal bipolarity.

Each human being is bipolar, that is, has in itself elements that are "M", masculine, active and "F", feminine, passive. Depending on sex, one or the other usually prevails. Both "M" and "F" elements have their own aspects which are positive and negative. We will try to list some of these characteristics.

MALE ASPECTS		FEMALE ASPECTS	
Positive	Negative	Positive	Negative
Courage, firmness, decisiveness, competence, sincerity, magnanimity, frankness, broad vision in creative work	Acerbic, authoritarianism, fanaticism, subjection to the inferior desires.	Femininity, swiftness, modesty, prudence, tenderness, scrupulousness.	Shyness, longing, indecision, falseness, cunning, dissimulation, sentimentality.

The student's work in the 2 of Coins stage consists of:

1. Discover and know the "M" and "F" characteristics of their psycho-animic being, learning to do well; between each other.

2. Try to overcome the negative aspects of both.
3, Practice successively the "M" aspects and the aspects "F", trying to develop its sides to the maximum positive. Tradition recommends that the student exercise frequently practicing for a set time, only aspects of a polarity, previously chosen. To do this, you must carefully analyse all impulses, feelings, as well as the way of acting; should cancel everything that expresses opposite polarity. By practicing it, the student will have the impression that he is no longer the same person. However, you must forget that this is just a soulful psychic exercise.

4. Develop the latent positive characteristics, especially those of the opposite sex. Generally, positive aspects of one of the poles are the opposite of the negative aspects of the other pole, for example, courage and cowardice; delicacy and rudeness.

5. To underline the "M" and "F" aspects, that is, to consciously raise the level of their handling. So, for example, when it comes to loving your neighbour, giving feeling in a more perfect and complete way, both under the "M" aspect as under the "F". Such sublimation goes beyond the psycho-soul level and has repercussions on the spiritual.

The elements "M" and "F", as far as possible, should be brought to the same level and polished against each other. Remaining delimited, they should be harmonised in your opposition. We underline that the "M" elements and "F" belong to a type of binaries that are not mutually exclusive but, on the contrary, they can agree very well.

The purpose of all this training is to develop as much as possible the two poles of the human being, so that, later on, carry out its harmonious synthesis. Achieving it, the disciple takes the first step towards overcoming psychological limitations linked to the separation of the sexes.

The conditional concepts "active" and "passive", in relation to the elements "M" and "F", the characteristics do not correspond to "active" and "inert", but define two different ways of acting. When the torus manifests itself openly and externally, it is called "active"; when it doesn't manifest on the outside, but acts internally, " passive " '. The card of the 2nd Major Arcanum, presenting the feminine principle, confirms it. The tiara covers the head of "Isís", and the veil covers her face. In other words, your mental and higher centres are hidden. The woman does not reveal the mental reasons for her actions, nor her final target.

In Eastern terminology, the element "F" corresponds to "Shakti", the hidden principle of Nature that receives, assimilates and gives form to the creative impulse, given by the element "M". M-F bipolarity is an analogy, in the lower planes, of the primordial vision of the One in two aspects. The only initiation of Cups and Wands symbolises the union of these two Primordial Aspects. The breast of "Isis", that is, the three psychic centres: the throat, the heart and the plexus are uncovered, indicating that in women the intuition and the heart are more pronounced. This feminine characteristic is so accepted that even the public opinion easily excuses the woman who let herself go and made a mistake because of feelings.

The lower part of Isis's body is hidden by clothes. The woman hides the activity of her lower centres, even when they play an important role in her life.

Traditionally, humanity requires that the woman is pure and chaste.

In the "M" principle, on the contrary, everything which is erased in "F" is accentuated. Creative impulses are manifested in the higher centres and the effort to perform them on the physical plane. The element of reason and logic is more pronounced, as well as the use of physical torus, both constructive and destructive, since there is a need to highlight the activity of the lower centres.

Let us move on to another corresponding Major Arcanum - the 11th, - which is the Arcana of Force. On the slide, we see a Wands which, without any fuss, opens a lion's throat. It's the power of the "F" torus, when spiritualised. This power is much larger than that of Samson, who splits the jaws of the lion. A good illustration of the power of these two modalities of force is the well-known tale about the wind and the sun. The wind and the sun discussed which of the two would get to take the coat off the pilgrim's back. The wind, though he used all his fury, didn't succeed, but the sun, warming up, caused the pilgrim to take it off willingly on his own.

The corresponding Arcanum, number 20 - presents, in the image on his card, a man, a woman and a child, leaving from a grave and rising to the top. The sublimation of "M" and "F" principles is the 'first step towards achieving in the future spiritual androgyny.

Two of Coins corresponds to Sefira of Wisdom - Chokmah and the Divine Name IAH. This Sefira is the first expression of bipolarity.

In alchemy, the two of Coins corresponds to the purification and magnetisation of the active and passive elements that will be used in the alchemical process.

3 OF COINS

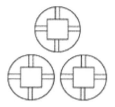

Correspondence: SEFIRA BINAH
Major Arcana: 3, 12 and 21

The number "3" can be considered as the most symbolic element of harmony, because harmony comes from the union of opposites and the trinity expresses the neutralisation principle. This is the unification of two elements in one.

Harmony, in turn, is the condition "sine qua non" of the entire creative-evolutionary process. It is because of this that all esoteric teaching systems are based on the trinary principle, and that this principle exists in every religion that has an esoteric base. In the Sephirotic system it is symbolised by three triangles of the Sephirothic Tree; in Hermetic Philosophy it is expressed by the triangle of the Archetype "EMESH", formed by the three Mother letters (see Major Arcana); in Ethical Hermetism - by the triangle "AGLA", representing the three types of souls.

In the previous Arcanum, the disciple had already separated, harmonised and sublimated its internal elements, "M" and "F". The task that awaits you in the 3rd degree of Coins is to unite them, creating the androgyne within you. This creation is symbolised by the ascending triangle, that is, the neutralisation of opposites, which allows one to reach a higher plane.

Seen from the upper planes, the ascending triangle also symbolises the descent and division of the Primordial Creative Force.

The analysis of the elements "M" and "F", practiced in the 2nd degree of Coins, is no longer needed in the 3rd degree and would cause only a delay in the formation of the complete human being.

Let us look in the Major Arcana corresponding to the indications about this formation.

The 3rd Major Arcana is that of the ternary, both ascending and as a descendant. The disciple must perform the neutralisation; to the ascendant, that is, the state in which the two polarities of internal forces come together harmoniously and creatively, when moving to a higher plane.

Esoteric wisdom states that nothing is created, that everything is born. This means that new internal content appears as a consequence of the conscious work done previously.

Realise the androgynous, internal state and be able to be governed by both reason and feelings; it is a broad view, but it is also precise in detail; be demanding and determined and, at the same time, understanding and prudent, etc., all depending on the particular case.

Little by little this way of being, self-imposed at the beginning, becomes natural, due to the fact that the nature of the disciple is already androgynous.

Being androgynous does not mean being indifferent or lukewarm, getting halfway between the "M" and the "F", but on the contrary, always adopting a clearly defined position, be it "M", or be it "F", as appropriate. Physical sex naturally influences work, and it almost always starts under a strong predominance of "M" or "F".

The creation of internal androgyne is a preparation for the future realisation of the merging of twin souls, that is, the two halves of the same Monad. The realisation of this merger requires, on the part of another, certain sacrifices. They must be conscious, voluntary and even incorporate an element of happiness (see Major Arcana

3 and 12). Any birth is linked to suffering; as also in the case of the birth of the Superior Androgynous Being.

It sometimes happens that certain details of the elements "M" and "F" do not fit in a harmonious way; then it is necessary to change what, in itself, may not be negative, but that prevents the harmonious synthesis of "M" and "F".

The 3 of Coins also corresponds to the Major Arcana 21. The main indication of this Arcanum, in relation to the 3rd degree of Coins, is intrepidity. In the world of "non-I" nothing can frighten or hesitate the pilgrim who took the initiatic path. No impediment or opposition, coming from this world, you can stop it. Your life should be governed solely by the determination to reach the final Reintegration.

There are rare cases of harmonious, innate bipolarity, in humans. It is a proof that a conscious evolutionary work [which has been accomplished in previous incarnations]. However, the most frequent case among human beings, is a disharmonious mixture of both polarities, with predominance of characteristics determined by physical sex. There are also, several types of polarity distortion, such as:

a) Androgyne, with a predominance of "M" or "F", created by a union of negative characteristics. It's a neutralisation of opposites in the direction of descent (involutive);
b) Polarity determined by physical sex, with almost total absence of the characteristics of the opposite polarity. Even in the case of developing good qualities, the person is one-sided and, in a sense, primitive. Such cases can be found among domestic animals;
c) Deviated polarity, with unilateral characteristics of the opposite sex. These are very rare and often linked to sexual abnormalities.

We will also add that the binaries that are not neutralised, neither in the top direction (for conscious work), nor downward (unconsciously), and that, therefore, remain binary, are manifested by constant conflicts of internal relations between the pairs of opposites involved, instability in the corresponding plans and a nervous breakdown.

The 3rd degree of Coins, which corresponds to Sefira Binah, concludes the first ternary that gives the system a basic boost.

The previous Arcanum, corresponding to Sefira of Wisdom - Chokmah - allowed that, through wisdom, perceive the single Principle as the Source of everything that exists, and that we understand the importance of the initiatic path. Sefira Binah is the Sefira of Reason. It's throughthe reason that the disciple can acquire the knowledge of his mental and psycho-soul being, knowledge that it will be indispensable to be able to harmonise and sublimate it.

Sefira Chokmah is the principle of knowing, Sefira Binah – the knowable field. Wisdom - Chokmah – attaches to a superior objective; Reason - Binah - indicates the means to achieve it, according to internal and external conditions.

In alchemy, the stage of 3 of Coins corresponds to the formation of the "Rebis" mixture. The active and passive elements that enter their composition, have already been purified and their qualities developed to the maximum, in the preceding degrees. This is how the "androgynous" and harmonious synthesis is formed: **"REBIS"**.

4 OF COINS

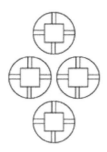

Correspondences: SEFIRA CHESED or GEDULAH
Major Arcana 4, 13 and 22 °

The task of the 4th degree of Coins is to carry out the quaternary - יהוה- in internal life (static quaternary) and external activity (quaternary dynamics). Since the 4 elements of the quaternary are often symbolised by the so-called "hermetic animals", the 4th Arcanum of Coins also received the name of Arcana of the hermetic animals.

In the 2nd degree of Coins, the disciple worked on the aspects "M" and "F"; in 4th grade you will have to work on the four "animals". The relationship between the four basic planes of the Universe, reflected in the constitution of the human being, and the four hermetic animals is as follows:

Mental Plane   Eagle
Astral Plane   Man or Angel
Physical Plane   Bull
Spiritual Plane   Lion, joining the 4 into one whole
                    and making the human being a self-
                    aware individuality.

The corresponding graphic symbol is the Cross of the Hierophant (see figure 7 in the following Arcanum), in which the vertical segment, which represents the spirit, unites the 3 horizontal into a whole.

The disciple's first work at the stage of 4 of Coins is to become aware of the existence of these planes or "animals" within and clearly delimit them. In practice, it means learning to analyse and classify all the manifestations of your inner life. The disciple will then discover that several "I's" exist in it, each with their own demands and desires.

Then you will see that, in addition to these "selves", there is some superior principle that you are able to observe in these "selves". It is also necessary to govern them, according to your conscious will, but also necessary to admit that you could have done so already if you hadn't been so weak.

The appearance, in human life, of this superior aspect of the "I" is already a proof of the influence of the spiritual plane.

After a clear delimitation of these internal planes, follows the stage of harmonisation of the lower three, of thoughts, of feelings and physical manifestations, which is nothing other than the subordination of them to the will of the higher aspect of "I".

This harmonisation could be carried out more easily by developing the positive characteristics of the four "hermetic animals" in each plane separately, as follows:

On the Mental Plane:

a) the mental range and correct relationship (Eagle);
b) the power of logic (Man)
e) the ability of thorough analysis (Bull)
d) the final synthesis, correctly elaborated (Lion)

On the Astral Plane:

a) the courage and speed of correct decision (Eagle)

b) the ability to govern their desires and traditions and submit them reason and will (Man)

e) perseverance and preservation of their internal world of alien invasion (Bull)

d) dignity in its convictions and subordination to the Superior Authority (Leo).

On the Physical Plane:

a) the speed and lightness of movements (Eagle)

b) the control of physical desires and appetites (Man)

e) patience in facing difficulties (Bull)

d) strengthening the organism and maintaining health (Lion).

The disciple needs to find out which of the hermetic animals predominates in it, what are its positive aspects and which negatives (the latter can take a very subtle form). Next, you also need to realise the degree of influences of other "animals", strengthen their positive characteristics and overcome negative ones, harming them all.

The positive and negative aspects of these "animals" are based on the elementary composition of the disciple Following:

ELEMENTS	POSITIVE ASPECTS	NEGATIVE ASPECTS
EARTH	Ability to create support fees on the physical plane, facilitating spiritual achievements, and using material possibilities for higher purposes	Predominant importance in the material aspect of life.
WATER	Ability to adapt to the accepted forms of the environment, preserving its internal independence.	Predominant importance in the material aspect of life.
AIR	Aspiration and spiritual elevation, accepted as reason and purpose of life.	Spiritual dispersion and tendency to ingenuous people and fantasies
FIRE	Fiery spiritual ardour (but in the psychic centres, which can have positive or negative consequences).	Attachment to all kinds of feelings and feelings

It is important to underline that the characteristics of the three lower planes (physical, astral and mental) can be improved with special exercises (see annex), while the state of the elements that make up the human being is the consequence of the spiritual level already reached and, therefore, the exercises they cannot improve it; can only develop the willpower. The evolutionary will, in turn, will influence on the ethical level of the disciple's life, which, over time, will cause certain changes in the elementary content. The elementary composition of the human being is symbolised by the cross with equal arms or "cross of the four elements".

In addition to the internal work on the "4 hermetic animals" (static aspect of the quaternary), the disciple must be active (dynamic aspect of the quaternary), that is, planning and perform a certain external, constructive work, in each of the planes.

In any work, whatever its character (philosophical, artistic, scientific, etc.), there are 4 phases:

1. General idea or the scope of the flight of the Eagle;
2. Planning the details and preparing the necessary material necessary (Bull phase);
3. Deductions and synthesis, as a result of the first two phases (Man phase);
4. Final completion of the work (Lion).

The majority of human beings go through these phases without becoming aware of them, but the aspirant for the Initiation must be conscious of each phase of their work. The introduction into the life of the four phases corresponding to the "hermetic animals" already shows an advancement on the initiatic path.

The Major Arcana corresponding to the 4 of Coins are all linked to the idea of realisation. The card of the 4th Major Arcanum provides guidance on how the job should be done. The "Emperor" openly applies his force and his will and based on reason (his face is visible). It is "male magic". The "female magic" (picture of the 2nd Arcanum) hides its force and reason (her face is veiled) and is directed by intuition. The "Emperor" leans on a cube, that is, something that has already been accomplished. So, too, should the disciple of Coins. The figure formed by the arms and legs of the "Emperor" - the triangle above the cross – indicates the mastery of higher principles on the cross of the elements, that is, it means the power to rule "hermetic animals", both inside and outside.

The titles of the 4th Major Arcanum: "Authority" and "Adaptation" point out an important aspect: each realisation constitutes a different mode of application, outside of itself, internal strengths and possibilities, through the 4 phases of dynamic law. However, each achievement must be done with maximum authority. The disciple must know his inner strength, to be sure that he has the right to act and, as in every magical situation, be sure of the positive results of the projected action.

The 13th Major Arcanum is the "Death and Rebirth". In relation to the 4 of Coins, this means that each realisation completed causes an internal or external change, either in the "I" world, as well as the "non-I" world; it also indicates that difficulties of the previous phase were overcome, leaving room for the new possibilities. In other words, it means the death of an old form and the birth of a new one. Pilgrims on the initiatic path can never remain stationary, but must continuously transmute their energies ("transmutatio virum "). In the Rosa-Cruz initiation, this law of renovation is expressed by the theurgic-magic formula "1.N.R.1. (Igne Natura Renovatur Integra) which means: by fire (spiritual) all nature is renewed, or even that the inferior man becomes superior.

In the card of the 22nd Major Arcanum, the "hermetic animals" occupy an important place. Note your evolutionary placement around the circle. Each completed achievement can be symbolised by an entire circle, but not a closed circle, that is, a fragment of the spiral. On the card, the Lion becomes the Eagle of the next cycle. the symbolism is the same as the snake, biting its tail, and indicates that in the spiritual path cannot be stopped, but it is necessary to pass from one to another hermetic victory. This is the basic teaching of the 22nd Major Arcanum.

In the Sephirothic Tree, the 4 of Coins corresponds to Sefira Chesed or Gedulah. This Sefira of Mercy, but also Organized Purpose, confirms not only that the energy must serve to reach a higher target, but that the means to achieve it must also be worthy of this target. On the other hand, this Sefira confirms that the work of the disciple should not be regarded as something imposed or unpleasant, but on the contrary, it should be a reason for happiness.

In alchemy, the stage that corresponds to the 4 of Coins, is the conclusion of the preparatory phase and the placement of the "Rebis" inside the "hermetic egg" to be subjected to action;

5 OF COINS

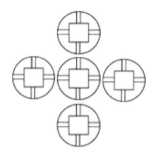

Correspondences: SEFIRA PECHAD OR GEBURAH
Major Arcana 5 and 14

The 4 of Coins dealt with the four present principles and active in humans. The 5 of Coins introduces a fifth and new element, the central, the "quintessence", or even the element SHIN or LOGOS (see 21st Major Arcanum). In the cross of equal arms, the graphic symbol of the quaternary, the Shin corresponds to the central point that joins the four arms. Adding the Shin to the divine name Iod-He-Vau-He, transforms it into Iod-He-Shin-Vau-He - יהשוה - that is, Ieoshua or Jesus.

The name יהוה could be interpreted as "Divine Will". The second word, having Shin (the Logos) as the central point, will indicate the means of manifestation of this Will. It is the symbol of INVOLUTION or DESCENT INTO MATTER of the Divine Word, to act on the physical plane.

In general, the pentagram in an evolutionary (upright) position, symbolises being human. The four lower points correspond to its psychophysical composition and the upper point - the Spiritual Principle that this composition will become in its immortal soul.

One aspect of the Spiritual Principle is the Divine Will. In the pentagram, which symbolises the human being, the Divine Will is represented by human will, and it can be considered as being the projection of the Divine Will about the individual soul. The human personal will differs from the Divine whilst not discovering its Primordial Source and it is not integrated into the Divine Will.

In the stage of 4 of Coins, the will constituted an impulse to reach a desired target. In the 5 of Coins there are various different types of will and various ways in which it reflects on the inner life of human PERSONALITY.

The disciple, at this stage of spiritual development, must first of all understand that the will, although it is a reflection of the Divine Will, is, in general, very distorted, because of the disharmony and imperfection of the envelopments of the internal human being that the Divine Will needs to cross before reaching human consciousness.

The graphic symbol of the Cross of the Hierophant illustrates the subject clearly. When there is harmony between the three planes - mental, emotional and physical - symbolised by the horizontal lines, the vertical axis - the Divine Will - can cross them in a straight line. If the planes, instead of horizontal lines, have slanted or twisted lines, however, when the vertical line crosses them it also warps, that is, the manifestation of the Divine Will is distorted.

If human thoughts are directed at evil, volitional strength will propel man to bad deeds; if the emotional body is under the influence of lower passions, the will shall take the decisions caused by this involutive state. In the event that the physical body is dominated by an addiction, as in Fig. 8, the will shall be directed to satisfy this.

The disciple must know that, working to harmonise his body envelopes, he not only performs the first few steps on the path of general spirituality, but also purifies the will, which henceforth will always be more able to express the Divine Will. Progressively, the will shall no longer be directed to the satiation of personal desires and will instead serve the higher self. However, following the Higher Will does not mean to drown out the voice of feelings or needs of the legitimate personality. This characterises Eastern and Christian asceticism, which condemns any desire or will and recommends killing the body. The way of Coins advocates the development of all positive aspects of the human being, governed by the **EVOLUTIONARY WILL.**

To obtain a good result, the student must carefully analyse their inner world, learn to know the character of their desires and, using his/her mental abilities, discern the evolutionary desires from the involutive ones, but also to differentiate the natural and useful from the useless and superfluous which disturb internal work. The important thing is that these desires do not control you, but that they are controlled by you and, at any moment, if necessary, can be overcome.

Especially dangerous are the desires which have become habits. The disciple, aspiring to initiation magic, must get rid of habits, whatever the character of the same. However, in the internal life of the human being there are trends that the evolutionary will must take into account and even sustain and direct. These are the creative trends, whether scientific, philosophical or artistic. They all enrich the personality. However, the evolutionary will must not allow them to degenerate into disharmonious manifestations. You need to make them subtle and use them as a means of spiritual progress. Each human being has his/her innate characteristics: the predominance of reason, of feelings, of this or that element, etc. The evolutionary will must take this data, taking advantage of its particularities, both for the development of a multilateral personality, as well as to straighten and harmonise the bodies or planes - the sleepers - horizontal crosses of the Hierophant's Cross. The analysis of the conditions of the penetration of the Divine Will in the internal human "climate", reveals a mutual dependence: The Higher Will, penetrating the internal "climate", makes it subtle and harmonises it, but on the other hand, raising the level of this "climate" allows for a "better penetration of the Divine Will. It is normal for the disciple, in this degree of development, to have difficulty adjusting his/her will to the Divine. An important task of the internship of Coins consists precisely of establishing a harmonious relationship between the Divine Will and that of human personality. The first Arcanum of Coins spoke of the need to be conscious in all your actions. In the fifth Arcanum, this same permanent state of consciousness becomes more penetrating, because the disciple must consider and evaluate the ethical aspects of each action and impulse. Ethical Hermeticism affirms that a conscious bad action is, in a sense, better than a good, unconscious one. This paradox, apparently amoral, underlines in itself the enormous importance of being aware of everything that you do, say or think, becoming accountable, that is, RESPONSIBLE for everything. It is at this stage that the disciple learns, not just to make a deep analysis of their actions, words, internal impulses and reactions, but also to accept responsibility for the same. The conscious human will, even when degraded or purely selfish is, STILL, a manifestation of **QUINTESSENCE** - the fifth essence -that is, of consciousness, which is a Divine Principle.

The Hierophant of the card of the 5th Major Arcanum symbolises the principle of consciousness and the Higher Will, present in the human being. The two figures before him, the positive and negative elements of one's own personality. The Hierophant blesses the first and threatens the second. The title of the Arcanum - "Sciencia Beni et Mali" – confirms the importance of always being aware of the ethical quality of everything which comes from the personality.

Tradition calls the 5th Major Arcanum "The Arcanum of Life", because in the field of Hermetic Philosophy this Arcanum corresponds to the understanding that the "Divine Breath" penetrates into all the planes of creation. The perception of this omnipresence creates in the disciple of Coins a new understanding of himself and the surrounding world. Find out that one lives to make it easier for the Cosmic Hangman (Universal Magnetism) that moves and connects everything (Natural Religion) to manifest itself with greater strength. The disciple must understand the fact - and not just understand it mentally - that the Divine Breath, as Principle of Life, is inseparable from Universal Harmony and that, therefore, the vital risk of each organism is proportional to the harmony of the elements that compose it.

The connection of the 5 of Coins with another Major Arcanum – the 14th - is evident. The 14th, is the Arcanum of the harmonious synthesis of personality. The 5 of Coins explains how this synthesis can be carried out under the influence of the evolutionary will of the human being. Arcanum 14 also deals with the transition of energy, that is, the transition from one state to another. In the field of Ethical Hermeticism, the transfer of energy is manifested through the transmutation of the lower human elements into superiors. The energy hidden in the human being is called "Kundalini" in the East and "Elixir of Life" in the West. In Ancient Egypt it was symbolised by the Caduceus. H. P. Blavatsky says in the "Secret Doctrine" that Kundalini is the Shakti force moving in serpentine line along the column vertebral column. It is a universal principle of life, present throughout Nature and which includes the two basic forces - that of attraction and repulsion - electricity and magnetism are their manifestations. This torus provokes a continuous adaptation; internal content to external environments, which, according to Spencer[4], forms the basis of life. It also causes the adaptation of the external environment to internal energy. According to the Upanishad definition, it forms the basis of transmigration of the Spirit, that is, of reincarnation.

In humans, this force remains dormant in the sacrum plexus, is unconsciously aroused in the sexual excitement and becomes active during sex. To be able to submit it to your will and keep it as a psychic force for the work to be done, chastity is needed, relatively, at least, that is, to maintain full awareness and control during sexual intercourse and, retaining the flow, make the Kundalini energy rise and accumulate instead of being wasted. For the success of any magical performance, for example, sexual abstention is absolutely indispensable.

Someone who, without failure, knows how to control this energy, can activate the subtlety of their bodies, that is, transmutation of the elements which compose them, beginning with the physical body that will become less dense. In turn, the harmonisation and subtlety of inferior bodies causes a natural awakening of the Kundalini. THE esoteric reason for chastity - the basis of all systems of the spiritual perfection - aims towards accumulation and purification of that force.

There are different methods and opinions about how to awaken Kundalini. Believers of orthodox religions, in particular, condemn any volitional act provoking your awakening. According to the religious conception, the hidden powers (which appear under the influence of Kundalini) must arise automatically as a result of general purification, as gifts of the Holy Spirit.

In certain Eastern schools it is the Master who opens specific centres of the disciple, when he considers him sufficiently prepared. In other schools, Kundalini awakening is left to the discretion and responsibility of

---

[4] Herbert Spencer is referred to, naturalist, philosopher, psychologist, anthropologist and British sociologist, from the 19th century.

the disciple himself and the result depends on his internal preparation and conscious will. There are special yoga exercises to speed up the awakening of the Kundalini. It would be wrong to think that knowledge of this belongs exclusively to the East. In the East, especially in India, this knowledge became more widespread via yogic schools based on the Patanjali system.

In the West, the study of the force called in the East "Kundalini" was limited in initiation schools. This study was part of the hidden wisdom of ancient Egypt and later of certain occult esoteric centres in Europe. The symbol of this force is the Caduceus of Hermes. This symbol, that can be considered as a synthesis of the Sephirothic Tree, presents the main characteristics of the force of Kundalini: The central axis – Sushumna Nadi, the two snakes - Ida and Pingala; the four points of intersection in the central column - the four chakras that correspond to the four planes, that is, the physical (lower point), the astral (the first crossing of snakes), the mental (the second crossing serpents) and the spiritual (the small sphere). The wings symbolise the general elevation as a consequence of ascent of the force.

Of course, occult powers, such as telepathy, clairvoyance, etc., increase the possibilities of realisation and enrich the personality of an aspirant to magical beginning. However, starting his work in that sense, the disciple must know that if he is not sufficiently prepared, the Kundalini awakening will turn against himself. Astral fire, one of the manifestations of this force, will act in a destructive way and may cause a psychic imbalance and even a complete loss of reason. Despite the importance of occult powers, the realisation of a 5th grade disciple of Coins is not to develop them but to establish an esoterically correct relationship between one's karma and the evolutionary will. The torus of evolutionary will shall determine the progress, but it is the result of two influences: That of the Divine Will and that of the personal will. Therefore, the degree of evolutionary will is also conditioned by the past, by all evolutionary and involutive activities that formed the disciple's current personality with its torments, weaknesses and nature of his/her desires, that is, conditioned by Karma.

The 5th degree of Coins is a reflection of the fifth Sefira, that of Severity, which, by the principles of order and legality, reasonably limits the Sefira of Mercy. The 4th Sefira and the 4th Arcanum expressed an authority and the will to action in the present. The 5th Arcanum deals with conditioning as a consequence of the past, that is, of Karma, conditioning the evolutionary will. This, in turn, will determine the future. This we will deal with the 6th Arcanum.

In alchemy, the 5 of Coins corresponds to exertion of the psychic energy of the alchemist-operator on the "Rebis" mixture. Psychic energy - corresponding to Kundalini - constitutes the quintessence of the process; it is the influence which causes the transmutation of the "Rebis" mixture in the "Philosopher's Stone". In alchemical language, this 5th force is also called "Nitrogen of the Sages".

6 OF COINS

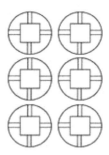

Correspondences: SEFIRA TIPHARETH
Major Arcana 6 and 15.

This Arcanum is the logical continuation of the previous two and refers to both internal work and external activity of the disciple.

At a certain stage of development it is advisable for the evolution of the disciple of Coins that they go back into the surrounding world again. An isolation for too long could harden your heart and damage the intuition. A period of self-analysis lasting too long, developing the principle of reason, could take place at the cost of sensitivity, which is also necessary. This is the first danger that the disciple encounters on the Way and that you need to avoid, instituting an adequate "modus vivendi" in your environment. Ethical Hermeticism teaches that it is preferable to take just one step forward and advance your environment – even a tenth part of that step - than to take ten steps, giving nothing to the environment. It is by giving that man receives. The spiritual understanding already acquired by the disciple, which is in the 6 of Coins stage, will preserve it from the opposite danger: That of being absorbed by the environment he seeks to raise. The disciple needs to neutralise correctly the binary: Isolation - relationships with the environment. The first tendency is a natural consequence of internal work.

the third danger, resulting from contact with the environment, can be the spirit of proselytism or dogmatism, that is, the desire to impose on others what one considers oneself to be the Truth. The disciple needs to cultivate the great quality of absolute patience and understanding and learn, in this sense, to adapt to the environment, to be able to transmit the Truth to each individual under the aspect that is more understandable and at the level that suits the individual.

The card of the 6th Major Arcanum presents a young man in front of the division of the paths and between the very different women; one of them points the way up, the other to the lower one. It is the allegory of choice. It is likely that this card has served as a theme for Titian's famous painting "Heavenly love and earthly love", where the role of the young person who must make the choice is left to the viewer.

However, for the 6 of Coins disciple, the problem of choice is different, because you will choose between "ascending" and "descending", that is, between evolution and development, when you took the spiritual path, confirming it, from then on, by your internal work. Now the choice is between personal progress and work in the environment.

How should you act? The answer was given above: You must neutralise the torque - internal life - work in the environment - finding the correct synthesis, that is, the middle path. However, Arcanum 6, Major and Minor, underlines the fact that the choice is not a separate and independent act in itself; it is conditioned by the past and, of course, will depend on it in the future. For this choice to be correct, certain conditions are necessary. Freedom of choice or, in general, to resolve to take any decision, leads us to the broader problem of free human will. Affirming that "the choice is free and the result predetermined", the 'esoteric tradition refers to the conscious personal free will and responsibility for consequences of that choice or decision. Subjectively, the agency is free and, therefore, inevitably subject to karmic consequences. The karma of the moment is the consequence of the choices and decisions made in the past, because karma and free will are closely linked.

It is worth asking whether the choice is also free in the sense of a goal. The answer is given by the content of the earlier Arcana of Coins: It is free (in the esoteric sense of this word) when it reflects the Higher Will, that is, the will of the higher "I", crossing without effort the wrappers of the personality. It is free when expressed as a profound determination and not as a personal and superficial desire. It is free, even when making decisions, considering personal particularities and according to those particularities. Truly free will can be only an evolutionary will, always conforming to the spiritual principle and, the more evolutionary, the freer it will be, because it will not depend on the small human "selves". The disciple needs to get rid of these "selves", not just in theory or in imagination, but in every gesture of daily life.

Knowing what the "legitimate" demands of your personality are, you will accept them reasonably and consciously, without however, identifying with them. Then you will become receptive to the will of your higher self. This is the basic work of the 6th grade of Coins and you can even say that the entire work of the disciple who took the initiatic path is, in reality, to become receptive to the Superior Will, establish it firmly in yourself and identify it with your own.

In the first grade of Coins the disciple learned to analyse and to discern the nature and origin of their desires; in the 6th he learns to have control over his decisions in order that they always remain free from inferior interference. At this stage of spiritual development it is very important to constantly remember responsibility for each proper action. In the 5th degree of Coins, the quality of the evolutionary will was to be understood as a result of past karma. In the 6th degree it must be understood as a factor creating the future.

This subject is very well illustrated by the "Mystic Triangle" of Fabre d'Olivet (see 3rd Major Arcanum) in which the binary - personal will – karma - is neutralised, to above, as the Higher Will - or Providence - which, in the human being, usually manifests as a voice of conscience.

Complementary explanations of the 6th degree of Coins can be found in the symbolism of the card of the 15th Major Arcanum. This symbolism, in relation to the Coins suit, acquires a new and esoteric depth. The astral divinity – Baphomet - symbol of the state of internal development of humanity as a whole, can also be seen as an image of being androgynous which, in its superior synthesis, expresses aspiration to the union of soul mates (see annex to the 6th Arcanum of Coins).

The 3 of Coins degree dealt with the internal androgyne. The subject of the external androgyne belongs to the disciple of the 6th degree, who has already learned of its bipolarity and worked to create the androgyne itself. Now, you need not only understand the teaching regarding soulmates, but make this matter a reality in your spiritual life.

In Christendom, the mystery of soul mates was expressed in the sacrament of marriage, which is something real when it represents a merger of two souls, not just one external ceremony. The Apostle Paul says: "The man will leave his father and his mother and will join his wife in one body; it is a great mystery." (Ephesians 5/31).

The merger of two incarnated human beings takes place naturally in the internal sense. Externally, they continue separated. However, a new common entity is created, which really exists on the supra-physical planes. It's the androgynous being created by them.

How can we find the "soul mate" among the multitude? It is a difficult task, as it is conditioned by the karma of each of the halves and, in general, the encounter occurs only when it has been predestined.

Esotericism, both Eastern and Western, teaches that the majority of human beings are karmic, that is to say, that we find the souls with whom we already have karmic ties, positive or negative, which considerably increases the possibility of meeting soul mates. When that happens, these souls recognise each other immediately, since the higher conscience, in both cases, penetrates even the personalities, although the two sides generally consider the meeting as a simple "happy chance".

A spiritualist must consciously aspire to this encounter, meditate on it, create its mental image, magnetising it with the will. Such mental concentration and volition can act as a magnet for this or a future incarnation, especially if the other half does the same as your side.

A specific case of the application of such a mental and volitional concentration is a magical appeal, addressed to the unknown soul. The magical power of this appeal creates in the astral world a vibration of a totally individual character, which provokes a reaction, almost always misunderstood, in the soul which has the same astral vibration, establishing an invisible connection. In case it is quite intense, according to Law, it will take place later on the physical plane as well.

Occultism admits another possibility: The creation of a hidden, artificial androgyne, with the proviso that there is a vibrating similarity between the souls. If the magic power of the operator is very strong he can adjust for himself a "soul soul", inculcating certain psycho-animic characteristics. Such an androgyne will be of a purely occult character and will not exceed the limits of his temporal personality. No one magician has the power to artificially create the spiritual union like the one that exists between true soul mates. Besides, the creation of the artificial androgynous has a dangerous side: the magician takes upon himself the karma of the soul transformed by him.

There is also another form of occult androgyne. This is natural and created by a harmonious union between two people of the opposite sex, as happens, for example, between a very close couple. Such an androgyne is created unconsciously by both participants and from the lower level planes, while the true androgyne originates on the spiritual plane, in the fact that they belong to the same Monad, which causes a strong mutual attraction of a supra-rational character, different from the harmonious synthesis of the personal characteristics.

The card of the 15th Major Arcanum has yet another androgyne variant, which is formed by the exclusive physical attraction of the sexes. The participants remain separated in everything that is on the physical and lower astral plane and, in most cases, are slaves of their passions. Such a relationship is very different from the true spiritual union and even includes the hidden androgynes (artificial and natural) and could be called the "sexual drug addict".

As a schematic of the realisation of the spiritual androgyne they can serve both sides of an ascending, regular triangle. Starting from the two lower ends, that is, the maximum distance, corresponding to the physical plane, the two sides of the triangle converge as they rise, to finally join at the top end. Indeed, the process of approaching soul mates progresses the measure that both rise through hierarchical planes. The physical bodies remain, of course, the most separated. In terrestrial life, unification begins with the creation of a common fluid, that is, of an etheric body and, through the plane of emotions and feelings, reaches the mental, creating the union of thoughts. In addition, it starts true spiritual fusion.

If we accept the division of the human being in spirit body, we can say that the sexual androgyne is formed by physical attunement; the occult by the harmonisation of souls and, often, bodies as well, and the spiritual covers the three planes, if in the physical we include the etheric, because physical union is far from indispensable for the realisation of the highest type of androgyne, especially when consciously created. It is rare that karma allows the matrimonial union between soul mates.

These various types of androgyne correspond to various types of attraction, commonly called "love". There exist also different ways of loving, from animal passion to the highest spiritual form. The latter is characterised by the total absence of self-centredness and the search for personal happiness.

In the case of a true spiritual androgyne, there is no predominance of one or another of the polarities in any plane. Neither of the halves leans on the other; each feels equally entitled to create the union. The two sides are not a mutual complement, as is the case of the occult androgyne, but they merge harmoniously on all planes. It is a mysterious process that could be compared to two harmonies that, uniting, create an even more perfect symphony. This fusion of two beings of the deepest sense is of great value for the whole life.

The realisation of the future spiritual androgyne can be conscious or unconscious. In the latter case, it is slow, almost automatic, taking place in the upper planes, outside knowledge of the people involved. The conscious formation, which constitutes a proof of [will be on the path of] Initiation is much more intense, especially if the two halves, not only aspire to their future union, but know the origin, nature and target of that aspiration.

What will the work of soul mates consist of during your stay on Earth? Creating the Spiritual androgyne itself is a divine work that, unalterably, exists on the spiritual plane, beyond any reach or human influence. Therefore, it's not about this.

To seek understanding, let us turn to the Bible. This tells us that there was a "fall" due to a rupture, which results in a separation between the Divine Flow and the "lower waters", that is, the astral substance. The work of twin souls will therefore consist of forming a common super-personality, free from the involutive elements of the astral, androgynous and perfected envelope, so that it can serve to address the Spiritual Principle. This work is a direct route to Reintegration and is carried out in all planes of personality. It starts with the creation of the common etheric body, as a consequence of the continuous contact of fluids, which can be intensified by special mutual magnetisation exercises. The common astral body is created by inter-penetration of the auras. The creation provided for the internal androgyne in each of the participants (see 3 of Coins) facilitates this merger. The solar plexus - place of emanation of the aura - plays an important role in this work.

Concentration on the subject made, if possible, in common, as well as certain meditations, because of the similarity in the way of thinking, form and strengthen the common mental body. Concentration, by both sides, on the thought-form of your androgynous being and of its vivification with vital fluids is an important moment of this occult work. Certain exercises facilitate this unification. As a consequence of all this, there appears the feeling of putting on a single heart and a sole conscience. Mutual telepathy is generally the result of the unification of mental bodies.

The more subtle the participants' bodies, the easier it will be to unify them, just as on the physical plane, the mixture of gaseous carp is faster than that of solids or even liquids.

On the physical plane, the body of the androgynous body is, of course, very relative, but the higher the plane is, the more this body is real, until it becomes an ABSOLUTE REALITY in the spiritual world. From a hidden point of view, the super-personality created is an etheric-astral formation, similar to an egregore. In reality, it is a specific egregore, composed 'of two beings. As in all egregores, its components are similar but not identical, they do not dissolve, but they enrich each other.

The impetus for the creation of the spiritual androgyne comes always from above and, as it forms, a large magical force begins to manifest itself in the joint performance. Several creative capacities are also emphasised, because the androgynous being, by approaching its source, becomes a direct transmitter of monadic emanations.

The spiritual androgyne, at the current stage of evolution of humanity is extremely rare. For this reason, this phenomenon is even more important for the general evolution. In the same way that an ordinary couple, very harmonious, has an evolutionary influence about their environment. The evolutionary influence of a spiritual androgyne goes beyond the environment, unfolding around humanity. Each spiritual androgyne, performed, is a tear made in the dark veil of involutive astral [energy] that surrounds the planet. It's an opening which allows the access of the Light.

In the symbolism of the 15th Major Arcanum, the realisation of androgyne corresponds to the passage through the Baphomet body to the flame that burns in your head, because Baphomet represents, as we already said, the total planetary astral, with a predominance of involutive characteristics.

It is natural that the disciple in the Coins stage still did not find his soul mate. It is important, however, that the image of the future encounter is alive in him, animated by thoughts, feelings and will. Thus, in your aura will form a magnetic field that will contribute to the approach, no one will be lost in that sense

In the Sephirothic Tree, the Sefira Tiphareth, which corresponds to Arcana 6 of all suits, is in the centre of the Tree, between the active and passive columns. The name - "Harmony" - indicates the harmonious neutralisation of opposites. In relation to the 6th degree of Coins, it refers, first of all, to the androgyne. In Sefira Tiphareth, almost all channels that reconnect the "I" world - the internal (column from the right) - with the world of the "non-I" - the environment (left column). We know that the "fall" of man affected the harmony and lowered the level of Tiphareth. Man, for his sublimation, for the correct use of free will and the approach of androgyne - the task of the 6th degree of Coins - can raise Tiphareth to the old level and restore enhanced primordial harmony.

The two Major Arcana that correspond to the 6 of Coins, the 6th and 15th, both have a connection with the environment. The graphic symbol of the 6th Arcanum is the hexagram. This one indicates the harmonious neutralisation of opposites: Isolation - work in the environment; effort to evolve – karmic limitations; "M" aspects - "F" aspects.

The titles of the 6th Major Arcanum are: "Medium" (medium environment) and "Libertas pentagrammatica" and mean that the work on yourself in the medium environment must be the best thing, in full harmony with you own will, with no external or internal imposition. If the work is experienced as an unpleasant task that one must undergo, there will not be the desired result. Imposition, if any, is admissable only at the initial stages of the initiatic path, when the evolutionary will, still new, needs to control the demands and involutive desires of the lower nature; when the spiritual and conscious determination "I want" needs to drown out the voices, still strong, of different "selves".

The work of the 6th degree of Coins is a consequence of the preparatory work carried out in the previous grades, and the symbolic details of the 15th Major Arcanum card allude to all these previous achievements such as: Awareness of Oneness (single flame above the head of Baphomet); development in itself of the "M" and "F" principles (Baphomet bipolarity); creation of the internal androgyne (ascending triangle, formed by two human figures and that of Baphomet); development in itself of the four elements (wings, terrestrial globe, scales and flame) and authority over them (cube); power of influence the environment, according to your will (straight pentagram on the forehead) and awakening of the Kundalini (Caduceus). This means that these realisations are a necessary preparation for the creation of the external androgyne.

In alchemy, the stage that corresponds to the 6th degree is the establishment of a harmonious connection between the spiritual principle and the fifth (in this case, the alchemist-operator) and the "Rebis" material. The operator must remain in constant contact with this matter (which corresponds to the environment), exercising its mental, psychic and fluidic influence on it, permeating it with his or her thought-forms, will and magnetism and, in turn, becoming sensitive to the vibrations of the "Rebis". In alchemy, this stage, in a sense, is decisive, because for the process of transmutation to begin, a connection between the operator and the "Rebis" must be established. If the process starts, but the connection has been interrupted, the process will stop.

The previous stages had a preparatory character, the 6th must manifest the result: The beginning of the process. How long will it take? It cannot be predicted, as nor can be predicted the pace of progress of a disciple. It all depends on the spiritual and hidden potential and the realising possibilities of the alchemist. It can only be said that the greater the potential of the operator, the faster the process. Below a certain level of this potential, the alchemical process of transmutation will not take place. This explains the cases in which alchemical operations were nothing more than purely external manipulations, without any result.

7 OF COINS

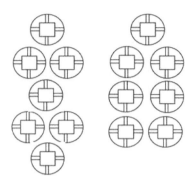

Correspondences: SEPHIRA NETZACH
Major Arcana 7 and 16.

At this stage, the disciple gets acquainted with the "7 Secondary Causes ", that is, in relation to our solar system, the 7 planets or, in Eastern terminology, the "7 Rays".
At birth, the influences of the planets print their seal, both in the internal content and in the standard of life that awaits the newborn. These influences can be studied on the "sky map", that is, the reproduction of the exact position of the stars at that time.
However, it is very important that the disciple understands that the entire astral complex is based not on chance, but on a karmic, logical and orderly consequence of his previous lives. He is born at a certain time because he deserves it and because he needs the experiences he is going to have. Studying your sky map will help you to better understand past mistakes and guide you on your path.
The discrimination between "good" and "bad" karma, in relation to external manifestations, belongs to the next degree, the 8 of Coins.

In the 7th degree, what matters is the karma that influences the internal human content, that is, everything in your life that will come from inside. To discover the character of his/her karma, the disciple needs to analyse the position of each planet, its aspects and determine which of the planets is dominant. The disciple's work at this stage will primarily consist of "purifying the planets", especially if, despite his previous work, he continues with the same weaknesses.

Now, you can look at them from a new point of view - the sevenfold - and you will understand the negative influences of certain planets, which need to be "purified". Then you will have to develop the positive aspects of the planets which are weak in your map, as well as the complementary planetary features. Thus, multilateral development will result in your personality that without it, even in the case of being harmonious, would remain one-sided and limited.

If the disciple is working to open one or the other of his/her psychic centres, they will achieve this more easily, helped by the strength of the planet that rules the determined centre. Tradition speaks of "governing your planets" and "spinning the planetary spectrum in such a way that the 7 planetary colours - or Rays - merge into white light ".

What does this mean? "Spinning the spectrum" means having the ability to rotate the 7 chakras or centres simultaneously. But, it also means knowing how to use in your life positive vibes from all planets, that is:

a) from the Sun, knowing how to organise and be efficient at social work;
b) from the Moon, being useful and appreciated at home and in the family;
c) from Mars, making quick and correct decisions and being energetic in action;
d) from Mercury, having an inventive spirit and adaptability;
e) from Jupiter, possessing well-founded authority;

f) from Venus, a soft and loving way;
g) from Saturn, a logical and serious way.

The dominant planet, also called "lord of the horoscope", is the most pronounced planet and constitutes, so to say, the "axis" of the personality, something more profound behind the personality, which could be compared to an IDEA that got involved in a personality. This allows us to pass the concept of INDIVIDUALITY. We have already talked about the 5th principle of the pentagram - the quintessence - as a superior principle, the Divine Spirit, potentially present in each soul and enabling Reintegration. Between the Divine Spirit and the human personality there are several intermediate states.

The first, that of the personality, is called INDIVIDUALITY. In Hebrew language, individuality is called "Haia" and in Eastern terminology, "superior Manas". Individuality participates in the formation of personality and, in turn, constitutes a denser envelope for the highest principles.

Individuality conveys an "internal hue" to the human personality. The character of individuality can be captured by observing the field in which one expresses oneself, the highest aspirations of human beings and their most profound problems.

Each human being, whose individuality is very pronounced in one way or another, incarnated to perform in his/her life "missions" that are in deep harmony and chorus with that same individuality. The subject of Messianic missions belongs to the 10th degree of Coins; to the 7th, belong the missions which are "coloured" by the individuality.

Individuality can also be manifested by artistic creativity, scientific research or philosophical works. The dominant planet determines the character of expression. However, the "dominant planet" should not be confused with the "horoscope ruler". They belong to two distinct planes. The "dominant" rules individuality and individuality, when sufficiently developed, presides over the formation of personality, which is one of its aspects. The "dominant" already characterises the spiritual elements; the "regent" - only the psychic-animic and physical.

The highest human aspirations generally belong to the religious field. According to the planet of individuality, 7 basic modes of expression of these aspirations can be distinguished:

a) The solar type will seek to illuminate and sanctify all aspects of life, introducing religion into all their manifestations and, sometimes, wanting to make it a dominant factor. This type is sensitive to beauty and brightness, the external aspect of the rituals, the grandeur of the temples, etc.

b) The lunar type will always be very attached to their religion, usually the one in which it was created, following rigorously its precepts and customs.

c) The Martian type will dedicate himself to proselytism, willing to sacrificing himself and even being martyred at the altar of his faith. Given to be missionaries and preachers.

d) The Mercurian type will seek to understand the truths and give them a philosophical basis, will like debates on these topics and will try to prove the good foundation of his faith. Apologists belong to this type.

e) The Jupiterian type will see in God the supreme and fair authority. Religion will be a law for him, governing the life of man and society. It will give much value to rituals. This type forms religious legislators.

f) The Venusian type will understand religion as a moral law, governing life and relations with the environment. He/she will try to help others, will work in social works and will be compassionate. Religious artists belong to this type.

g) The Saturnian type will see in the language a linguistic teaching the mystery of the presence of God in human beings, will live in spiritual solitude, in isolation, being able to become an anchorite. This type gives religious philosophers and abstract mystics.

It is necessary to underline, however, that certain internal experiences, such as, for example, from living a deep love of God or others, to purely spiritual manifestations, are above any individual tone, although they can express themselves in different ways.
The 7 basic types, listed and delimited above, constitute only a general pattern. In reality, several of these influences exist in each human being and in degrees more or less accentuated. Each individuality is unique, there are no two alike, just as on Earth there are no two identical people. In each incarnation, the elements of personality, purified and harmonised, absorbed, in essence, by individuality and enriching it.
In the "spinning of the planetary wheel", in the creation of the synthesis, these individual shades do not disappear, because that would mean the total loss of personality achievements. They harmonise and remain, forming a unique solar synthesis.
Often, individuality is not yet manifested in the human being; other times, it already manifests, but in a way distorted by the lack of harmony existing in the personality (see the Cross of the Hierophant). In the religious field this can be expressed as fanaticism, exaggerated asceticism and purely external, without any spirituality, or, then, as an attachment to only external expression of the realisation. In social life it can give despots, people looking for personal glory, flattery, etc.
The distorted manifestations of individuality are, sometimes the consequence of some failure on the initiatic path during the previous incarnation, due to which the individual principle had to get involved with distorted elements.
In the spiritual principle - and individuality already is - there can be neither positive nor negative aspects, such as happens in the personality. Individuality is always

"whole", "individual", that is, indivisible, because by the nature of its vibrations, it belongs to the higher planes. However, it can only manifest itself through personality, that is, through the astral and physical plane.

This is the reason why harmonisation of personality – the channel through which superior influences may flow into the world - is indispensable. Especially important is the harmonious relationship between the planet of individuality - the dominant of the personality - the conductor. The vibrations of individuality, for example, of Martians, will need to find it in the composition of personality, the means to express oneself broadly and harmoniously. If they do not find it, the individual expression, which in any case will keep the Martian character, will be misrepresented.

Individuality is sometimes called a "permanent atom". It is the part that does not die in the human being, that returns to the terrestrial plane, involving each time in a new personality. In each incarnation, individuality collects the most sublimated elements, the most harmonious essence and, for that very reason, more permanent of the personality.

These elements, passing to the individuality, become super-personal. esotericism does not accept survival of the personality, as manifested on Earth. What survives the "post-mortem" stages of disincarnation more is personal. The immortality of the soul, in the sense of keeping the permanence of consciousness through incarnations, corresponds to the transition from personal consciousness to individual consciousness. The terrestrial personality cannot be immortal, because what is not harmonious, or only partially, cannot be permanent, and also because, in each incarnation, the personality and the physical body are again formed of the astral substance. However, due to Karma there is a bond that unites successive personalities. Sometimes, this bond remains through a series of incarnations, as a chain formed of causes and effects. Yet, it is more pronounced between two successive incarnations.

Karma determines the moment of birth, under the influences which, acting at that moment, will condition the new personality.

A disciple of the stage of 7 of Coins, as we said, needs to not only harmonise personal content, but also to discover the character of their individuality, analyse the elements of the same and strive for it to become more possible. This is the basic achievement of this degree. All the disciple's internal work must be dedicated to his individuality and he needs to know that this job is the fight for their immortality, a struggle for the identification of their personal conscience with individual conscience. Realising the identification, the personal will that drove the work of the disciple's inner self, will become the will of individuality.

Let's look at the relationship of 7 of Coins with the Major Arcana correspondents. The 7th Major Arcanum is the Arcanum of Victory. In 7th grade of Coins is the disciple's victory over his internal planetary conditioning. The "Winner" is the individual principle who, in the disciple, becomes master of the psycho-soul and physical being.

The card of the 16th Major Arcanum, in relation to Coins, symbolises the collapse of the personal, inferior elements, under the knowledge of the higher will.

The 7 of Coins Connection with Sefira Netzach, Sefira of Victory, is evident and needs no comment.

Netzach is also the first Sefira - in the downward direction - of the last triangle, the triangle that is determined by initiation.

The 7th degree concludes the septenary of internal experiences and initiatic achievements of the disciple of Coins. The characteristic common to the achievements of these degrees is that they are all the results achieved by the disciple's own efforts. It is the part of the initiation work done "from below upwards ", it is the" climb ", without which it would not be possible to receive what comes "from above" and which will be the theme of the three last grades of Coins.

The first seven degrees correspond to the Seven Secondary Causes, the last three to the Three Primordial Causes. The 7th degree of Coins synthesises all personal scents of the disciple. In alchemy, the operator, also synthesising all of his volitional, psycho-mental and fluidic emanations, seeks to impregnate alchemical matter with them. Connection between the alchemist and the "Rebis" has already been established in the preceding grade; however, the two still remain separate and the influence that "Rebis" absorbs continues to come from outside, that is, from the alchemist. When that absorption reaches its maximum, the last part of the alchemical process will become possible.

8 OF COINS

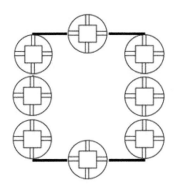

Corresponds to the SEPHIRA HOD
Major Arcana 8 and 17

The graphic symbol of the 8 of Coins presents two equal
squares, having a common centre and that we must
imagine spinning, as if around an axis, in opposite
directions. These squares symbolise the active elements
of the process of the Creator who, in the human being,
acts so much from outside to inside as well as inside
out.

These elements, in the East are called "Tatwas" and, in
Western esotericism - essential and substantive
elements of everything that exists. They are elements of
the Universal Creative Force that has two aspects: "the
one who creates" and "what is created". The Biblical
Elohim and all that was created by them represent
these two aspects, that is, the essential (creator) and the
substantial (created).

The human being is unaware of the external tactical
forces that they create. It is conscious, when the forces
are those which he himself creates, according to his will.
In humans, in general, only the four lower tatwas -
"Prithivi", "Apas", "Vayu" and "Tejas" - are manifested,
and each side of the squares corresponds to one of

those tatwas. The common axis of the two squares represents the fifth tatwa, "Akasha", which links the lower four tatwas to the two superiors: "Adi" and "Anupadaka", not manifested in the human being. Tatwa Akasha manifests itself, sometimes partially. Tatwa Akasha conveys the two aspects of his/her force to the human being, through the four lower tatwas. Akasha's influence, acting through the Prithivi tatwa, governs the organic, natural growth of each physical organism, from birth to adulthood and also causes the complete renewal of your cells every seven years.

Acting through the Apas tatwa, Akasha governs development of the etheric body; through tatwa Vayu, the astral body and through Tejas - the mental body, that is, intellectual capacities. In every normal human organism, these four tatwas are active. It is necessary to underline that, of those four, the lower two - Prithivi and Apas – are the beginning of the substance, while the two superiors - Vayu and Tejas - remain in a state of force.

The tatwas are the seven aspects of the Universal Creative Force - the seven planes of the creation - from the highest to the lower, the physical. The complete work of the seven tatwas, takes place only in the Macrocosm; in the human microcosm, in general, only the lower four tatwas are manifested.

Both the tatwas and the planets are the Seven Secondary Causes of the World and the relationship between these two complexes of forces can be compared to the relationship between the content and the mould that shapes that content. Tatwas create, planets shape what is created.

The unique and inimitable essence of each individuality is created by Akasha. The shape is given to that individuality by the dominant planet. The strength and the development of individuality depends upon the degree of Akasha's manifestation in humans. In the same way as in the case of the manifestation of Individuality through the planetary complex, the more developed the four lower tatwas in humans and more harmonious the cooperation between them, the easier and broader will be conditions for Akasha's manifestation.

Manifesting itself in a pronounced way, the Akasha tatwa can act directly on the content of the personality, even to "implant the seeds of the Spirit in it" and serve as a conductor for the upper tatwas.

The direct action of the Akasha manifests itself as a general spiritualization of the personality, starting with physical and ethereal bodies, guiding the development of hidden psychic forces, intuition and expansion of consciousness. Unlike what is normal, such a development, although there is no conscious awareness of the person in question, could be called occult and esoteric. It is the internal work of the Spirit that cannot be provoked, nor accelerated, nor routed in one or another determined direction. It can only be verified with gratitude and whilst trying not to hinder the process due to some internal disharmony.

Tatwas, by themselves, just like planets, are neither positive nor negative, but the tactical force changes in an unharmonious or distorted way when there is disharmony in the personality. Tradition teaches that upper tatwas can manifest even as destructive force if the lower tatwas - that is, the personality –not being harmonised, resist higher vibrations. This is usually expressed as a total loss of control over desires and emotions, revolt against any authority and accepted forms in the environment, as well as by destructive impulses. However, this spirit of denial and destruction is not caused by the aspiration to create something new and better, which characterises the Swords experience; The intent is to deny and destroy. On the other hand, it is not a problem of primitive vandalism, a problem of stupidity, but of a revolt against the imperfection of life forms and against your own inability to change something.

Pausing in this matter, we want one more time to highlight the absolute need for purification and harmonisation of the personality before any other spiritual work.

The simultaneous rotation of the two squares of the symbol of the 8 of Coins, in opposite directions, symbolises the two aspects of creative process:

1: The "involutive", that is, the immersion of the subtle in the dense or the "that which creates us" aspect.
2: The evolutionary, when we consciously make the more subtle dense, that is, when "we create ourselves".

It is important that the disciple is aware of the existence of these two aspects of the process and their interdependence.

Let's look at this second and very important aspect, that is, the conscious and creative work of the disciple, which in the 8th degree of Coins is related to the tatwas. The work of tatwas is a little different, as it does not consist of "purification", as was the case with the planets, but in reinforcement, that is, to raise their vibrations, because each tatwa has a full range of vibrations. It is possible, for example, to make subtle the physical body in such a way (a substantial aspect of tatwa Prithivi) that this, by itself, will activate the subtlety of the psychic content, thus increasing the superior receptivity. This is the explanation of the esoteric value of fasting.

One can consciously work to develop the personal magnetism (substantial aspect of the Apas tatwa) or to sublimate the psychic and mental elements (tatwa Vayu and Tejas); (see annex to the exercises and special regimes). The disciple needs to be aware of the degree of development of their tatwas, in order to raise their vibrations.

To achieve harmonious development and balance between mental power and the ability to feel deeply, the two planes - the mental and the astral - must be simultaneously developed areas. Likewise, they need to be simultaneously developed from the two lower - the etheric and the physical - so that their vibrations are not only not specious, but even facilitate the subtlety of the elements of the superior personality.

All the disciple's previous work on himself was an indispensable preparation to be able to consciously raise the vibrations of their essential elements (mental and astral) and substantial (etheric and physical). The action of the four lower tatwas can be twisted through personal, conscious work and appropriate exercise. The action of the 5th tatwa - the Akasha - the spiritual principle, cannot be twisted by the disciple's own effort, but it is possible to create conditions for the same to manifest with more intensity. The Akasha tatwa manifests itself in several ways:

1. As universal support of life, causing growth and the development of each living organism. In that aspect it acts through the lower tatwas, which emanate and merge into it. In the plant world, Akasha acts through dais tatwas (physical and etheric plane), in the animal world through three tatwas, physical, etheric and astral and, in the human, through the four tatwas. The human being, as has been said, is not aware of this tactical action.

2. As a creative force, felt by the human being and manifested as "evolutionary will". This manifestation is comparatively rare, as it covers only those who consciously seek to evolve.

3. As a creative team, directed to the world of the "non-I", it is the manifestation of individuality in the scientific fields, artistic, philosophical, etc., fields dealt with in the Previous Arcana. According to its grade, the force manifests itself as a skill, talent or genius. These are gifts that cannot be attracted by their own efforts but can be developed or wasted, according to its application (or lack of).

4. As strength that spiritualises the personality, participation in that sense of the person in the body. It is the result of intense internal work in a previous life. This strength is super conscious.

5: As a manifestation of the "Spirit that blows where it wants". They are in superior states in which everything that belongs to personality disappears. These states, in general, are not part of the Coins suit, but of the positive aspect of the Swords and even of the higher suits, because they are experiences lived by those who united their will to the Divine Will. They are manifestations of supra-conscious strength and will go directly to Initiation.

The 8th grade of Coins concludes the esoteric teaching about individuality which is also often called "the real me" and that is always more pronounced as the disciple advances on the initiatic path

The 8th grade of Coins also includes teaching about the three types of souls, named after three letters of the Hebrew alphabet - Aleph, Ghimel and Lamed - and that together form the divine name AGLA. The numerical value of this word is 1 + 3 + 30 + 1 = 35, which, by adding the figures, gives the number 8 (see the 8th Major Arcanum). These three types of souls correspond to three different paths towards God:

1: The Aleph type conceives of God as an abstract, transcendental force and seeks to approach Him through knowledge that is scientific or hidden. It is the way of philosophers, scientists and metaphysicians.

2: The Ghimel type follows the path of divine immanence, through internal, super-rational experience, the divine presence in itself and to feel a part of God. It is the path of mystics.

3. The Lamed type also has a transcendental conception of God, but achieved through intuition. He will feel the Divine Life in all creation and its journey for God will be that of union with Nature, of love and compassion for all

beings, as children of the same Father. He will be ready to sacrifice for the good of everything and, arguably, a religious pantheism.

The last letter - Aleph - from the divine name Agla, is the union, on the higher planes, of these three types of souls, the one that belongs to the Wands stage. The differentiation of human souls in three types corresponds to the triple division of the Monad in higher tactical planes

Every soul that is not exclusively limited to materialism, that is, which is open to higher influences and not spiritually degraded, belongs to one of these three basic types that, in reality, are the expression of three spiritual currents. Each of these chains flowing through human individualities is expressed in different amplitudes and different spiritual depths, acquiring a unique, unrepeatable expression. You can say that a "fragment" of one of these three currents gets involved in the determined individuality, as the same involves the human personality.

The disciple in the 8 of Coins stage needs, not only to identify their soul type, but also to ensure that it can manifest itself as perfectly as possible, through their individuality and personality. If your personality is not sufficiently purified, it will reflect in the Aleph type in the form, for example, of narrow dogmatism and the attachment to scholasticism, in the Ghimel type as the experience of illusory astrals and in the Lamed type like a species of unconscious "dilution" of individuality in the environment.

The 8th degree of Coins is also related to the teaching on the Three Major Causes, whose graphic and kabbalistic symbol is the "Triangle of the Archetype", that is, the triangle of the divine name "EMESH" (Aleph, Mem, Shin). The numerical value of that word is $1 + 40 + 300 = 341$, which, adding the numbers, gives 8.

In relation to Ethical Hermeticism and the Coins stage, the Three Primordial Causes are expressed as follows:

Cause **ALEPH** - as a specific character of individuality, reflecting one of the three types of souls. Individuality, of which the disciple perhaps has not yet become aware, manifests through personality in the specific character of his aspirations and the way in which the disciple, consciously, creates themselves.

Cause **MEM** - as a spiritual influence that comes from on High and that "creates" the disciple, if he, by previous conscious effort, prepared his internal content to receive this superior influence. It is the spiritual strength that, acting from outside, through Akasha, can transmute the human being, ready for this transmutation.

Cause **SHIN** - as the force of the disciple himself. Without it, no creative work would be possible, despite the existence of aspiration. It is the presence of Akasha, magnetised in the disciple, which allows creativity.

In the preceding grade, the 7th, the disciple needed to overcome the negative aspect of internal karma. The 8th grade task is learning to govern your external karma. Conduct it, which means learn to face positively all events, all external aspects of your life, using them for your spiritual progress. Nothing happens by chance, everything has its reason for being. A necessary trial, if repelled, will return again. All events and situations must be constructively taken advantage of and not become reasons for an involution.

The 8 of Coins corresponds to the 8th Major Arcanum. The graph symbol of this - a square of Coins, inscribed on a silver square - represents the same idea. This variant stresses the difference between the two forms of the creative process: The Coins frame symbolises internal work, the silver one - external influence.

The three titles of the 8th Major Arcanum: "Libratio", "Karma" and "Lex", refer mainly to karma. "Liberation" in the aspect of Coins, is the realisation of the karma balance and will, without which the Initiation would not be possible!

The other two titles are reminiscent of the law of cause and effect and the inevitable consequences of everything that has been done. In addition to the divine names mentioned above, Tradition links the 8th Major Arcana and, therefore, the 8th degree of Coins, to the third divine name: יהוה (1 + 5 + 6 + 5 = 17, giving the sum of the digits - 8). This name, in relation to the 8 of Coins, corresponds to the creative work of the four lower tatwas, taking place from top to bottom (4) and from bottom upwards (4), that is, in eight aspects.

The other corresponding Major Arcana - the 17th - is the Arcanum of Nature. The force of this, renewing life, is nothing other than tactical strength. Arcanum 17 deals with help received from on high. In the 8 of Coins aspect, it is the superior tactical influence. The Arcanum titles - "Divinatio Naturalis" and "Signum" - refer mainly to astrological conditioning, closely linked to karma. It is an element of astrological determinism, rectified by the element of indeterminism, expressing itself by the well-known motto: "The stars incline, but do not compel".

Realising it is a test of discipleship and the 8th degree of Coins indicates in what conditions this can be done. The third title, "Intuition", confirms the gift of supra-intellectual knowledge, given by Akasha's action.

Finally, the title "Spes" indicates that before the disciple who performed the purification of the 7th degree and became aware of the work of tatwas, the possibility of Initiation, that is, of the spiritual birth to a new life. On the spiritual plane, hope, that is, the conviction about the future, is one of the highest manifestations of intuition.

The 8 of Coins corresponds to the eighth Sefira, Hod, Sefira of Peace. In all suits, the 8th grade is a grade that refers to the internal work, that is done in silence and that transforms the human being. In Cups is the mysterious influence of Akasha, transforming the disciple and preparing him for the Initiation in the next degree

In alchemy, the 8th grade of Coins corresponds to the more spiritual stage of the alchemical process. The "Rebis" mixture, inside the "egg", has already received the maximum external influence. Now, the alchemist concentrates all his mental torments and volitional strength (the "nitrogen of the wise") to act on this mixture from the inside and the "Philosopher's Stone" is born in it. This alchemist's spiritual strength, acting on the elements of "Rebis", corresponds to Akasha's action on the inferior tatwas, present in the human being.

Rebis Theoria Philosophiae Hermeticae, Heinrich Nollisus

9 OF COINS

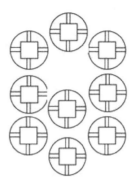

Correspondences: SEFIRA YESOD
Major Arcana 9 and 18

The graphic symbol of the 9 of Coins is the figure called the "Grande Arcanum of Initiation" (fig. 9), which is composed, in turn, of three different symbols: Above is an ascending triangle; in the middle, a hexagram; at the bottom, a square over the cross of the elements and circled. The totality presents the numerical value: 3 + 2 + 4 = 9.

This pantacle can have different specific interpretations, but always represents Initiation in the three planes: The spiritual or superior, the astral or medium and physical or inferior. The pantacle can refer to esotericism in general or to one of its ramifications, such as, for example, Magic, Kabbalah, Alchemy, etc. as in the figure. In this study it will mean Initiation on the path of Ethical Hermeticism, corresponding to an internal flowering and the development of a certain realising power. We will deal only with the esoteric aspect of the

Coins initiation as the exoteric aspect is dealt with in the 9th Major Arcanum.

The Beginning of the Coins stage, differentiating itself from superior suits, does not correspond to a state, consciously lived, of supra-rational lighting that, for itself, transforms the human being. It is more like the conclusion of a prolonged process of spiritualisation in which, however, the supra-rational principle participates, of the interrelationship between the personal, consciousness of the disciple and the penetration of the Superior Force in him.

The Initiation of Coins is, therefore, not simply the sum of all achievements achieved by the disciple but more than that, because it gives birth to a new "unity", a new being. This being will not remain stationary, because the influence of the Initiation is always dynamic. A stop on the spiritual way would mean investment.

Each esoteric initiation has two aspects. On the one hand it is a confirmation of the level already reached; 'and the static aspect. On the other hand, the dynamics of the evolutionary process. Each Initiation, too, has its particular character, since the process of initiation is always deeply individual and closely linked to the disciple's unique individuality.

The 9 of Coins peak, as already said, is the symbol of each esoteric initiation, regardless of the evolutionary level and the individuality of the initiate. In relation to the Coins stage, it can be considered as representing the disciple's achievements in each of the three planes. Let's analyse these achievements in their two aspects: the development of internal power and the realising power. Start first at the upper triangle, which corresponds to the individual principle, that is, to the real "I", above the personal elements. According to the degree of its development this "I" becomes will manifest as personality ruler, as superior judge (voice of conscience), as an evolutionary will, as dominant planet, as a creative principle, as tatwa Akasha or as an aspect of the Monad.

The presence of this triangle indicates that the disciple
has learned to neutralise the binaries "in the top
direction", that is, to find a correct solution for all
opposites, abstract or concrete, that appear in life,
especially those of karma - will, the elements "M" and
"F" and, also, which aspire to the external androgyne.
The synthesis of these initiation achievements results in
an expansion of consciousness and in mental harmony.
The hexagram corresponds to the relationship with the
environment, in this case, the relationship of the
disciple's internal being, with your own personality. The
hexagram is composed of two equal triangles, but with
different placement. The descending triangle
corresponds to the work of the disciple relating to
his/her personality; the ascendant - their aspirations.
The disciple must balance these two aspects and
become "a harmonious hexagram". the development of
one of these aspects, at the expense of the other would
not give good results.
In addition to its general symbolism this hexagram can
also represent several particular aspects, such as, for
example, the harmony between karma and will, between
"M" and "F" elements or between planetary influences.
In the latter case, the entire hexagram corresponds to
the dominant planet and each line of the figure, to one
of the other six planets. Building "his hexagram", the
disciple learns, for that's right, also to build "its
superior triangle".
The set of the upper triangle and the hexagram can be
considered, in the initiatic path, as representing,
respectively the Three Primordial Causes and the Seven
Secondary Causes. The first correspond to the Objective
in name from which the Path is being trodden; the
second, to the means used by the disciple to achieve
this objective, that is, to decide his internal personal
relationships. So, this would represent the relationship
between the purpose sought and the means to achieve
it. In the case of achievements, personal activities
constitute, by themselves, the total or a part of the

desired purpose, the ascending triangle disappears and the Way loses its initiatory character.

The bottom of the pantacle - the square over the cross of the elements and within a circle - refers to realisation. Once we are analysing the pantacle only in relation to the disciple's internal state, the square represents what "the tatwas created within him" and the cross, "that which the "disciple himself created". The square symbolises the passive aspect, the cross, the active. The circle, around, symbolises the infinite or spiritual principle (or Akasha), acting from within and without. The cross and the square also represent the יהוה law, in their aspects: Dynamic (the cross) and static (the square), or also, the 4 "animals" or Hermetic virtues.

Let us now analyse the Great Arcana's beginning in relation to the realising power of the initiate, that is, their work in the environment. We have already spoken of the spiritual end that should encourage internal work. Let us now see on behalf of that, as and under what conditions the Coins initiate can perform an activity in the environment.

The upper triangle indicates that the "bearer of the strength and knowledge", that is, the initiate, can act only with higher ends, aiming solely at the evolution of the environment. This triangle must "be visible" to everyone, which means that by inculcating the Truths received from a Superior Source, the initiate must not hide the principles in name they are working on.

The hexagram refers to the methods of work. Both triangles - the ascending and descending - by themselves, already indicate two directions at work. Tradition adds to this hexagram two arrows in opposite directions, indicating that the triangles, in motion, change their descending to ascending and vice versa, symbolising the passage simultaneously from the subtle to the dense and from the dense to the subtle, that is, the descent and the ascent.

When the initiate presents, for example, the great Esoteric truths in the form most accessible to their environment, or transmits its force or its magnetism, "he descends", but his "descent" results, at the same time, in spiritual elevation or "raising" of the environment. This is the explanation of the movement of the hexagram. Another example of "descent" and "ascent" is the initiate's task to sublimate and expand students' awareness, making them understand the spiritual essence of what, until then, existed in them in the form of ideals or convictions. All of this makes the hexagram.

The "involution" of the initiate is essential to the evolution of the environment and that is why his work in the world of "non-I" is considered as "sacrifice" (see the 12th Major Arcanum).

Finally, the hexagram indicates that the initiate, in his work, must adapt to the evolutionary level of the environment. One could be receptive to the highest Truths in any form, others could only hold together the highest forms of those that are in turmoil. These are highlighted in the words of Jesus: "You are given the knowledge of the mystery of the kingdom of God; but unto them that are without, all these things are done in parables." (Mark 4:11).

The initiate, therefore, must have great discernment and take into account not only the evolutionary level, but also the psychology of the environment. On the other hand, they must be very attentive not to vulgarise the Higher Truths too much. One needs to find a harmonious solution to always raise the internal level of students.

The work of the initiate is not limited to transmitting certain initiatory knowledge. In addition, he needs to act directly on the conscience of students, temporarily taking possession of it and transmitting something of his own conscience. So, after the separation, the student's conscience gets deeper and richer.

Tradition teaches that, at the time of physical death, the consciousness of the initiate merges with the consciousness of only one of his disciples, the chosen one, and transmits "his Great Arcana ", thus continuing his spiritual life in the body of that disciple. For this to be possible, there must be between the two, the initiate and the disciple, a spiritual affinity.

We pass to the lower part of the Great Arcanum's pantacle, which refers to the possibilities and conditions of work of the initiate on the physical plane. They basically depend on three factors:

1. The support received from the egregore to which the initiate belongs, regardless of having this egregore manifest on the physical plane or existing only in the astral.

2. The social situation that the initiate occupies and which can facilitate spiritual work, such as, for example, a professor, in relation to students; a priest of higher degree in relation to the faithful, etc.

3. The purely material possibilities that, too, can facilitate your work, giving you, for example, financial independence, more time to devote to spiritual work, travel possibilities, etc.

When the peak of the Great Arcana of Initiation refers only to magical work, it is called Great Arcanum of Magic" and provides the basis for magical performance in three planes. This subject belongs to another course and we will dedicate to it here just a few words:

1. The top triangle, called "suspension point", corresponds to the theurgical part of each White Magic. It consists of the "confession" of the magician, the invocation of Superior Forces, the request for help, etc.

2. The hexagram corresponds to the magical force generated by ceremony and acting on the astral plane. This force depends on the magician's own power (the ascending triangle of the hexagram) and the strength of the clichés, magically permeated, as well as the formulas and conjurations, that the magician

implements, as well as the ritual instruments used in the performance (the descending triangle).

3. The lower part of the symbol corresponds to the "support "of the magician on the physical plane, that is, the magic circle and its proper preparation.

Let us move on to the corresponding Major Arcana, that is, 9 and 18, both linked to initiation.

The card of the 9th Major Arcanum, examined in all its details, characterises the life of the initiate, stresses their isolation, the darkness that surrounds him, the qualities he needs, the inner Light possessed, etc.

The 18th Arcanum card presents a still darker picture. It is the state of the world in which the initiate will have to work: Opposites not neutralised and which have not yet reached their definitive shape (two truncated pyramids), the blood of crime, desperate conservatism (crab returning to its time), the darkness in which the sun does not penetrate, etc.

The initiate's task, in this environment, is to play the role of the "Moon", which reflects the Light of the Invisible Sun, that is, the task of transmitting to humanity "Sun light". However, this role carries a danger: The environment can be attracted not by the pure Eternal Truths (the "Solar Light"), but by the personality of the initiate who transmits them; causing people to believe in him, follow him. This is the case for many great religions and religious movements, whose spiritual teaching was eclipsed by the adoration of its founder. It is the cult of personality which, in general, is unconsciously promoted by the most dedicated followers.

The same card also highlights other dangers that the initiate encounters on his way: Hidden enemies and false friends. The first are the result of ancient inner disharmony, which could arise from the depths of being, destroying the work of the initiate. The second - the small temptations that seem harmless, but that sometimes end up dominating the evolutionary will.

It is necessary to add that such eventualities are possible only at the Coins stage, where the personal and self-will still exist, despite having been put to spiritual service. In the higher stages the personal principle remains totally outdated; only the spiritual principle is essential for human beings.

The 9 degree of Coins corresponds to the Sefira Yesod. The Initiation is nothing but the realisation of a NEW FORM OF CONSCIOUNESS that originated in the feeling of Oneness (Keter), achieved harmony (Tiphareth), obtained the hermetic victory over personality (Netzach), was determined for internal work (Hod) and received a new form (Yesod).

Our exposure to the Coins path would be incomplete if we failed to mention a purely psychological factor that always accompanies the working disciple: A sense of inner happiness, that does not depend on external circumstances and does not resemble other joys of terrestrial life, because its nature is different, it is esoteric. It's one happiness that arises due to the awareness that one has of an internal growth, results achieved at work, overcoming weaknesses. This happiness increases more when the disciple realises that, he is helped in it by the upper, external forces.

In alchemy, the experience of Initiation corresponds to the birth of the "Philosopher's Stone" or "Red Stone" which, in reality, is a red powder. Its appearance is the supra-rational way, in the field of chemistry, as that is the physical experience in relation to psychological states, studied and classified by experimental science. So much that one, like the other, belongs to a Higher Reality. The Philosopher's Stone represents, in nature, the strength of the internal alchemist. It is a palpable density of this force. With that, the process ends. The alchemist can pass to multiply the "Stone" and make the Coins.

10 OF COINS

Correspondences: SEFIRA MALKUTH
Major Arcana 10 and 19

At this stage, the initiate of Coins already knows
his/her individuality, their forces and the internal
Spiritual Principle; knows the dangers of the Way and
knows where upon the Way they find thcmselves. Now
they can get to work, that is, to raise the evolutionary
level of their environment, whether this is the circle of
its students or society where they live.

The evolutionary level depends on two main factors: The
mental horizon and ethical principles. The initiate will,
therefore, have to work on these two senses.

From an esoteric point of view, widening the mental
horizon does not mean spreading general knowledge -
this is the task of a school of education - but rather, to
bring awareness of esoteric principles, create bases for
the development of esoteric thinking, as well as
transmitting certain knowledge of esotericism.

Ethical concepts, inculcated by the initiate, should,
also, have an esoteric basis and contribute to the
collapse of false morality created by the conditioning of
the past, morality that limits and corrupts human
society. It can be said that all the external work of the

initiate is a neutralisation of the binary: Personal internal content - level of the environment you work in. To give an idea of the possible diversity of the work to be done by an initiate, sketch your general character and the way in which it can manifest. Take the mentioned torque: Initiated (active pole) - environment (passive pole). Analysing the active pole, we will find that:

1. The spiritual level and the internal strength of the initiate naturally plays a decisive role, because the bigger it is, the more you can elevate the environment. One's spiritual level depends on the depth of the ideas and concepts exposed.
With regard to internal strength, the greater it is, the more it will be felt by those who have not completely lost their ability to exercise spiritual discernment. This explains why the same words that, in general, leave listeners indifferent, can have a tremendous influence when delivered by a possessor of the spiritual torus.
2. The individuality of the initiate will determine the FORM your job will take.

In the previous Arcana we talked about the two modes of creative work: The "top to bottom", which corresponds to giving Higher Truths in a way that is appropriate and accessible to the understanding of the students and the "bottom up", that is, a presentation of these Truths, according to the progress of the students, always in their higher aspects, that is, always less and less veiled by form.
Depending on his/her individuality, the initiate will choose one of the three basic modes of work, which can be called in the following way:

a) spiritual aristocratism;
b) spiritual democratism;
c) combination of the previous two.

It is evident that these denominations are totally relative, because all spiritual work is "aristocratic" and prevails in one the superior values of the human being. They are also "democratic", because the spiritual origin is the same for everyone and the perfection potentially belongs to each one. However, an initiate of the "aristocratic" type will be attracted to "create for the superior" and the "democratic" type will try to make the truth more accessible to a larger number of people. These tendencies, of course, influence the way of working. The initiate of the first type will avoid public meetings, will choose his students and work with each one individually or, at most, in small closed groups. Generally, nothing is done to attract students, as he will be convinced that the souls which have matured will come by themselves, from one or the other mode. He will accept only serious and hardworking students, teaching through private conversations and individual spiritual direction. This type also includes initiates who do not practice organised teaching, but that, by their answers to the questions, for their constant readiness to help those in need and, above all, for their strength and harmony with which they uplift all those around them spiritually. A simple encounter with such an initiate can change completely a human life. If such an initiate writes a book dealing with spiritual matters, that book will be understood by few, but it will have a large influence. The same will happen with any work of art, in which the initiate incorporated a spiritual Truth.

The initiate's work of the second type will have a very different modus operandi. Wanting to spread the spiritual teaching among the human masses, he will simplify it to the maximum, will enjoy each occasion to speak and will found wide movements of spiritualists, accessible to all. Their students, or rather, followers, will be helpers at work and representatives of their organisation. Their writings will have a popular character and, more often, will be handouts and not books.

It is not up to us to say which of these types of work is more useful. They form a binary, completing and completing both their tasks. The first retains the intrinsic Tradition and trains new instructors, the second raises the level of society or a part of it. However, don't think that initiates who work individually, with either chosen disciple or in small closed groups, do not influence the life of society. On the contrary, this influence exists and is sometimes important, as such people generally belong to a cultural elite that influences the life of the country. On the other hand, "Democratic" initiates, speaking to large human masses, in addition to arousing the interest - even if it is superficial - of those who may never have heard of the subject, reach the sometimes more prepared people, who will be able to take the initiatic path.

Analysing the individuality of each of these types of the initiated, we can deduce that the dominant planet of the first is Saturn (mysticism, internal isolation), or the Moon (principle of protection and tendency to limit the field of its activity to those closest to him), or even Venus (the idea enclosed in artistic works). The dominant planet of the second type will be the Sun (desire to be the centre of extensive social activity), or Mars (fiery preaching, capable of igniting the hearts of the people, concentrated activity in a given direction), and even Mercury (capacity to adapt to the environment). As for Jupiter, his presence as a planet of authority and hierarchy must be pronounced in both cases.

The third type of initiate, bringing together the two types, has the greatest possibility of carrying out an extensive and profound spiritual work. This type belonged to the founders of great religions, like Moses, Buddha, Jesus and other great Initiates. All of them, in addition to teaching the people, teach esoterism to the elect. There is evidence of such in the work of Buddha and Jesus with his initiated disciples. As for Moses, He left a very evident example of Discrimination in

Teaching: For the People – Synaptic Legislation - and
the entire codex of religious rules in several chapters of
the Pentateuch; for others, probably some Levites, a less
accessible teaching, that is, the mystical Kabbalah
(linked to Tarot) and the initiation subtext of Genesis. It
is evident that all these Initiates had already passed
through the upper stages of the Wands suit.
Let us move to the other pole of the analysed torque,
that is, to the environment in which the initiate works.
In this case, the term "medium" will mean both the
human masses, as some or even one disciple. Of course,
the lower the "environment", the more concentrated will
be the work of the initiate. In relation to the masses, the
work of the initiate provokes always a reaction, because
it implies the way of life of the people, with their routine,
their concepts and their crystallised habits. There are
several types of reaction:

1. Passive reaction that could rather be called absence
of reaction, as it is limited to just listening to an
initiate's words. Most men, even those who practice the
precepts of a religion, are so absorbed in their daily
problems that any appeal to a mental hitch or the
introduction of a new element in their life slides over the
aura, without it penetrating.

2. Negative reaction. In every society there are beings
actively opposed to esotericism, both because of rigidity
and limitation of their religious concepts and their pure
materialism.

3. Positive reaction. In this there are several
subdivisions:
a) Truths penetrate the conscience, causing an impact,
but they are not applied in life.
b) Truths penetrate the conscience, leading to an inside
job, especially a purification and harmonisation of the
personality. During that period, the person acquires a
new cosmic vision, but the internal Spiritual Principle

does not reach be discovered. These people can be called followers of esotericism, but not yet "disciples".
c) The penetration of truths and internal work lead to the initiatic path, that is, the inner spiritual experience. In each environment, this group will be the least numerous, but will prevail for its value. They are the "disciples". A "disciple" can work alone or under the direction of an instructor.

The choice of the type of work for an initiate depends also on the character, the composition and the ethical and intellectual level, environment, factors to which the initiate must adapt his teaching. Of course, adaptation will be much more painful the lower the level of the environment.

In each work initiated in the surroundings, an integration is established between the sides - those of the binary poles - in each one of these poles alternatively from the passive state to the active and vice versa state. The active state of the environment may also be manifested by a purely hidden aspect: Trust. This increases the spiritual strength of the initiate and, in a certain sense, "nourishes" it. Equal phenomena occur in relation to the egregore. The initiate creates, "nourishes" and makes it vibrate with its spiritual, magnetic emanations and its work in the environment. Vibrating, the egrégore, once again in turn, supports and fortifies the initiate.

The work of an initiate of Coins, for the evolution of the environment, is symbolised by the Jack of the Logos OR the realising aspect of the Logic Force or Universal Creative Force. Using the Tarot language, the initiate, by his contribution to turning the Universal Wheel, consequently reduces the long process of continuous incarnations and disincarnations, indispensable to the current evolution of humanity

Let's analyse the card of the 10th Major Arcanum, in relation to the 10th Arcanum of Coins, that is, the work of the initiate in the world. The Wheel rotates in the evolutionary direction, therefore, the work of the initiate to hasten evolution, stimulates his movement. Two figures are dragged by the turning of the Wheel: One going up, another going down, but both progressing in the evolutionary sense. They correspond to the two modes of work of the initiate. The two figures present imperfect elements, which means that esoteric truths, in transmission and adaptation to human understanding, lose a part of their purity and depth and, at times, are left misrepresented. The Sphinx, above the Wheel, symbolises the יהוה Law which governs the work and also symbolises the 4 "hermetic animals" or the motto: Knowing, wanting, daring and being silent. The Caduceus, which represents the initiate, emerges from dark sea waves, that is, the environment in which he works. the Caduceus axis rests on the concave of the wave and shape, with it, the figure of Lingam, symbol of fertilisation. It is the spiritual fertilisation of the environment by an initiate's work.

The card of the 19th Major Arcanum - Arcanum of Ethical Hermeticism - analysed under the aspect of the 10 of Coins, underlines the fruitful character of the work of the initiate. On the card, the sun's rays, touching the earth, turn to Coins. It is the Spiritual Light, transmitted by the initiate to the environment, which creates Coins. It is the alchemy that takes place in sensitive souls touched by the influence of the initiate. The children of the card represent participants in this process.

The symbolic figure of the 10th Arcanum of Coins, formed by the traditional ten coin arrangement of "Coins", an ascending triangle, presents, in the direction of descent, the numerical value 1, 2, 3 and 4, and corresponds to the יהוה that governs all directorial work. In Ceremonial Magic, it is represented by the evocation triangle, drawn before the magic circle and around from which, according to the Magician's will, appear the magical materialisations.

The law יהוה, in relation to the work of the initiate is expressed by the following phases: Iod - the initiate, due to the status reached, is able to move onto the work; He - comes into contact with the environment, forming this basic binary with it; Vau - an interaction is established between the poles, which results in a certain form of work; second He - the work is done.

The 10th and last Arcana of Coins corresponds to Sefira Malkuth, traditionally called "Kingdom". This Sefira is directly connected, through channel 22, with the Sefira of Initiation, Yesod - and it is a logical consequence of it. The initiate does not have the right to withdraw from the world and close in on him or herself. **One must act externally and if you do not do this you will lose your initiatory power**. The name "Kingdom", given to Sefira Malkuth, underlines the duty of the initiate to create this "Kingdom", not only in yourself, but also in your environment. This will be the "kingdom" of the egregore, created by the initiate and vibrating in tune with its spiritual and individual tone.

Sometimes Coins are called "Circles". It is the magic circle of the initiate, in the centre of which he finds himself. In this small "Kingdom" the whole "Circle" is organised. About the initiate is the Spiritual Hierarchy, to which he submits fully. Below is the environment, which he nourishes with the strength of initiatic wisdom. The internal world is in complete harmony with the external work. **The goal of the initiation of Coins is that the human being achieves harmony between his spiritual aspirations and his terrestrial life, working for Earth's evolution**.

Just as the Coins initiate uses his strength and his wisdom, creating "hermetic Coins" in human Cups, the alchemist completes his work, creating material Coins. The initiate of Coins began their external work, verifying their torments and their possibilities; the alchemist, for his part, is sure of the value of the Philosopher's Stone he obtained.

In the same way that the initiate of Coins seeks to increase their influence on the environment, so too the alchemist, before starting to manufacture Coins, multiplies the transmutative force of the Philosopher's Stone.

The Coins suit is the first stage of the journey. It is through it that the climb to the Fountain of Light begins. Therefore, whoever aspires to the Light, must first cross the suit of Coins, in this or another aspect, in this or another level, slower or faster, all depending on his/her previous achievements, their evolutionary will and individuality. The Coins experience is indispensable to be able to pass to the superior stages, generally to Swords.

It is indispensable, but still not enough, because the transition takes place only when the personal successes of Coins no longer satisfy, when their illusory character is apparent and when the initiated disciple starts looking for something more real. In consequence, the Coins stage is passed as a result of an internal crisis, which is none other than the beginning of defeat of the personal element. This crisis increases and widens slowly.

The very natural satisfaction that accompanies the external and internal achievements (for example, a positive transformation of character), could become a danger if it was too pronounced, as it would hide the continuation and the incessant ascent of the Way. A very successful artist with his work will not seek more perfection and will stop on the way. The disciple-initiate of the Coins who is satisfied with themselves, even interrupts their initial process, often until a future incarnation. The Spiritual Principle, for its nature, is dynamic and cannot remain inert. It is like fire - it *is* fire - always alive, always moving to the top. Worse still, if the disciple considers his growth held in Coins, as a merit. He would then completely lose contact with the spiritual element and the initiation will take on a purely magical character, that is, of "hidden Coins". That happens when the Spiritual Principle is poorly developed in the disciple and personality elements predominate.

Exceeding the Coins stage is proof of a very high evolutionary level, because the understanding of relativity of earthly successes is caused by the awakening of Spirit. Moving beyond the Coins stage, the human being leaves behind the world of human idols and relative truths, to aspire to the Absolute Truth and seek it. The departure of the Coins suit can be caused by the conscience of the illusory character, either of the world, or of its personality, facing a Higher Reality. The first case is more common when reason prevails; the second, when the mystical principle and the heart are more developed and the sufferings of the world felt by the disciple as always more and more acute.

The first leads to a revolt against the world, against the evil and the suffering that exist in it and against the Higher Forces that allow it; the second, to an almost total depreciation of the self. It is important to underline that this internal crisis, even when it manifests itself as a revolt against Logos, creator of the world, comes from the growth of the Spiritual Principle.

These two ways of leaving the Coins suit correspond to two ways of crossing the suit of Swords that, conditionally, are called "negative" or "philosophical" and in a "positive" or "mystical" way. In reality, the two are positive, therefore, both during one and during the other way, the personal elements are dissolved and replaced, progressively, by others, impersonal and spiritual, more limited by shape.

SWORDS

Philosophical or Negative Aspect

Swords is the suit of the "psyche", that is, of the astral and the mental, and your experience is lived when these two principles of human beings achieve the greatest development. At the philosophical or negative aspect of Swords, reason predominates above feelings or the heart.

This step corresponds to the "Nasham" plane of Judaism or "Manas" of Eastern philosophy. In it, the mental, having not reached the upper plane, "Haia", or "Budi", is not yet qualified for a creative synthesis, but only for an inexorable analysis that penetrates to the roots of existence.

The disciple, initiated in the hidden and magical aspect of Coins, already has a high degree of knowledge of his/her PERSONALITY. Having developed the psychic centres and magical abilities and having obtained a certain power about the astral world and its environment, they became able to create new forms and transform existing ones. Their activity is entirely governed by their personal will, which totally dominates the world of desires and emotions. He/she achieved the maximum development of personality.

However, simultaneously with these achievements, arose in their heart a dissatisfaction with the achieved, a depreciation of world values that, until now, provided so much contentment. Doubts about one's usefulness does that. One starts to aspire to something different and higher, becoming aware of the existence of a Light that permeates the world and wanting to discover its nature and its source. One hopes to be able to meet God face to face, to understand the human being and one's internal "I" - the reflection of God.

The Coins Initiate has the possibility to create something in the world, to offer something, but nothing else can be received, because he/she already has what the world can give. They still did not understand that, continuing to give, they would continue to receive, maybe something unexpected and different, because in giving it *is* received.

Having reached the maximum of personal power, he/she begins to realise the illusory character of the world. They are knowledgeable of the forms, but have not yet penetrated the essence that is hidden behind them, in the Source that creates them and, therefore, rejects them as only illusory, which affects them deeply, because the world around them falls apart. They admit the existence of the Creator Principle - the Logos - but, at the same time, perceive the illusory character of every servant. They see the sufferings of the world, note that nothing can change, despite all their personal power. They do not understand the purpose of such a world of suffering and injustice and a great revolt against the Creative Power is born in them.

Swords, in their negative or philosophical aspect, signify the stage of deep spiritual crisis that must be crossed and overcome, so that a magician, initiated from Coins, can reach the heights of the upper hermetic suits.

As we have already said, we are presenting in this course the higher level of the human path, through the Minor Arcana, that is, the level that leads to Initiation. However, in many people's lives there are the same steps at lower levels and they also need to be overcome so that evolution can progress. Such steps are presented, sometimes, following the degrees and suits of the Minor Arcana, sometimes in a different order. They can be short and they can last a lifetime or even several incarnations.

Spiritual progress, most of the time, follows a spiral line, returning the person to the same stages, but at a higher level. Generally, human beings do not have awareness of being tested by a certain suit or grade. On the other hand, one should not forget that not every deep revolt or scepticism is proof that the person is living the good experience of Swords; most frequently it is the consequence of some failure in life, manifesting itself in revolt, scepticism and animosity.

Many people consider themselves "atheists" because their intellect rejects the exoteric presentation of God or because they are experiencing a painful crisis; others follow scrupulously the precepts of a religion, removing from their mind any religious problem, so as not to fall into doubt. It's possible that the former are at the threshold of Swords, while the latter have not yet reached the suit of Coins.

The negative aspect of Swords is the source of almost all religious myths. The fall of the Angels in the book of Enoch, the revolt of the Asuras, in the Stanzas of Dyzan of the Secret Doctrine of Blavatsky, the Prometheus sacrifice that stole the heavenly fire, the temptation of the Bible serpent and many others have the same basis. The negative Swords experience is expressed by a very complicated internal state. Being the mental aspect, in this stage, the most powerful, man intends to unveil the mystery of life and its own being through the intellect. For him, the only criterion of Truth is his own mental power. He rejects any claim of authority, religious or philosophical. The limited and conditioned in the human being seeks to solve the problem of the Infinite and the Absolute. This results in failure and causes a revolt that can take very different forms.

This revolt and the active struggle against the Creator Principle of the manifested world, are gradually transformed into a search for the cause of causes and absolute values, that is, in a search for God. In each deep and widely lived experience of the negative stage of Swords, these two factors - the revolt and the search - are present.

The tetralogy of the "Ring of the Nibelungs", by R. Wagner, is one of the most expressive images of the negative aspect of Swords, their struggle and, at the same time, search for the Divine. Wagner also wrote the libretto of his operas and, in this work that took him many years, reflected about every sound and every word. The librettos of his operas are much deeper than is generally thought. It IS a "Mystery" and not just a theatrical "cycle".

In creation of his work, Wagner used epics and Germanic legends in a very free way, to present, in the background, mythological legends of the Nibelungs and the antagonism of material and spiritual principles, the genuine esoteric path of the human soul (Siegfried) that fights for its immortality. At one point, Siegfried, to be able to unite to his divine principle (Brunhilda) must disobey the creative power (Wotan) and break with his sword the spear of Wotan (symbol of the laws established in the world).

The sense of this symbolism is that, in his/her evolution, on the way to the union with their higher "I", the human being must reject everything that was achieved (during the Coins stage) and advance solitarily, regardless of any law or order, without the assistance of Heaven, without an authoritative conductor, obeying only their internal criteria, refusing any limitation and even fighting against upper interdiction. It is the path of incessant struggle, provocation by internal loneliness and desolation.

In this darkness, man needs to find the right direction and follow it to the end. If you lack the will to take it further, you may fall into the spiritual doldrums, into complete negativity or despair, from which there will be no way out. Aware of this danger, all the founders of the exoteric religions prohibit the knowledge of Good and Evil, hide the Heavenly Fire and prevent this shortcut to a set of laws, punishing the disobedience.

These protective measures have their reason for being and were established for the vast majority of human beings who need to rely on the magic force of forms and authorities in order to evolve, that is, to carry out harmonisation; the personality. For this majority, the absence of support points would result in internal helplessness. There are few who have overcome the need for such support and that, without falling into the internal void, are able to rise into a genuine spirituality, following the painful path of Swords, because suffering is the essence of this stage. However, without Golgotha, there would be no Resurrection.

Man, crossing this stage, rejects and denies everything, until the very beginning of life, for, finally, in the last degrees, finds God within the self. Progressively it frees itself not only from the illusions of the physical world and of the astral plane, but also of the last illusion: that of the principle who, in himself, denied everything.

In the Minor Arcana, this path is symbolically presented as an ascent through the sephirothic system of Swords, that is, the progressive sublimation of consciousness as the disciple[5] rises from Malkuth to the Keter.

---

[5] Even if the human being follows the initiatic path, he has passed through one other Initiation, he continues to be a "disciple", nevertheless, of a higher degree

ACE OF SWORDS

SEFIRA MALKUTH - THE KINGDOM

The image that corresponds to this Arcanum presents a
sword, standing, with the point directed upwards. The
handle is formed by a cross with equal arms - the cross
of the elements - and the card has the form of an
ascending triangle, very acute. A channel, along the
side, joins the cross of the handle with the point,
indicating the possibility of direct ascent from the
physical plane to the Higher Spiritual World.
Later, in the last degrees of Swords, this will also serve
as a channel for the passage of a flow in the opposite
direction: The descent of the Cups influence. Thus, the
symbolic image of the Ace of Swords, of a similar form to
that of Ace of Coins, reveals the essence of its suit itself
and alludes to the ways of crossing it.
This symbolic presentation shows that, to the extent
that the human being rises through the steps of
Swords, he or she moves away gradually from the
"realities" of Coins, or that is, the cross of the elements.
It also indicates the possibility to climb the acute path,
the most direct, because the channel represents the
central column of the Sephirotic system.
Its base - Sefira Malkuth - corresponds to the
manifested world, that is, to the world of the elements

or, still, to the lotus of four petals, of oriental symbolism. The direct ascent leads through the Sephiroth Yesod and Tiphareth, that is, through from the world of forms and the world of creation to the summit of the column - Keter - the Higher Spiritual World. The Ace of Swords is the first degree, the basic level of a new stage of the initiatic path. It corresponds to the break of the Coins Initiate with the "Kingdom" that he himself built on the physical plane.

King Solomon, with his wisdom and great magical power can serve as an example of an initiate who performed the Coins stage but did not pass it.

An initiate of Coins, having reached the maximum of hidden development and terrestrial power, discovers the illusory character of all its achievements. He aspires now to other values - the absolutes - and their powerful aspiration isolates him from everything that until now constituted his world. As a disciple of Coins he followed a master, he belonged to a teacher, practiced rituals, accepted traditions. Now he is totally isolated. His/her solitude is complete and nothing indicates the direction to follow. His or her own blindness during the suit of Coins seems to be self-deception; they abandon the external forms now deemed lies and limitations and repudiate the thought patterns of the Coins stage. Internal disintegration and emptiness are consequent, which characterise the negative aspect of Swords and increase with each step. They are nothing but a form of protest against the world, as it was created. The disciple loses faith in Creative Forces, finds no explanation for the sufferings of the world, everything seems wrong, cruel and useless. He denies the wisdom of the Logos and is determined to fight against Him.

However, despite his internal desolation, all efforts and aspirations of the disciple are always directed by a Superior - but an *unknown* Superior. It is a search for the Absolute, but he/she seeks without faith, without inspiration, without inner Light. Only will and thought sustains them.

As the disciple rises and frees him or herself from conditioning, the ascending triangle of the card becomes always narrower. He who rises rejects progress and, consciously, all their "points of support" in the lower levels, despite not having any "point of suspension" above. The card itself, in the shape of a triangle, very thin and acute, symbolises aspiration and mental concentration that now govern the life of the disciple, his determination to achieve an understanding of the mysteries of the world and its own existence. He is ready to leave everything if he does not discover a high purpose in the creation of the Universe.

This internal state of intense aspiration, of "taking over the city", finds its expression in Gothic architecture. The needles of the Gothic cathedrals seem to prick the sky, like a sword point.

The Swords stage, like the Coins stage, can be processed over the whole life or even during several incarnations.

In very rare cases, the entire path of Swords can be traversed in an instant. It's the instant elevation via the cutting channel, a very dangerous alternative, since the human structure may not be able to withstand a spiritual change that is so abrupt. The transfiguration of Gethsemani, with blood, sweat and the acceptance of the "will" of the Higher Will, can be considered as the sudden passage through the suit of Swords.

The Swords experience is exclusively internal and deeply individual and therefore only the basic steps of the suit can be sketched. The rest depends not only on the disciple's individuality and personality, but also the level at which he is living his experience.

Fully lived, it prepares and enables, in last degrees of Swords, the descent of the beneficial spiritual force, suitable for the Cup suit.

2 OF SWORDS

SEFIRA YESOD – FORM

The image of this Arcanum features two crossed swords, with the points directed upwards. It is the symbol of unresolved binaries, of the opposition between the disciple and Logos. However, despite being crossed, both swords point upwards.

Tradition considers that the sword that comes from the right - active – side represents the disciple, the one on the left, the Logos. This picture symbolises the "celestial struggle", of which, in its cosmic scale, speak all religions and mythological legends.

The first Arcana of Swords corresponded to the complex Psychological state which led the disciple, initiated in Coins, to the rejection of the world created by the Logos and the decision to oppose His work. The second degree determines the way in which this decision will manifest itself.

First of all, the protest takes on a passive character: The disciple refuses to participate in any constructive work. We must not forget that, as an initiate of Coins, he had the power to harmonise his environment, was considered a collaborator in the Logos' creative work, as a director of His will, as the "Jack". The Coins Stage ended by a deep internal crisis, by the realisation of the world's incurable evil and the conviction that any work would be useless and meaningless.

Having realised, as an initiate of Coins, an internal harmony, the disciple reacts with an exceptional force to the disharmony of the external world, painfully feeling his inability to change whatever it is he wanted. He comes to the conclusion that until now, he has either followed the wrong way or the system that is ruling the world is wrong, because of each other being mutually excluded. This psychological complex naturally results in an opposition of disciple to the Logos, an especially passive opposition, in which, however, there is an active aspect.

In relation to common humanity, the disciple has reached a much higher level. He got used to looking at the world from the point of view of those who participate in its development. This view logically entails an appreciation and a criticism; in turn, criticism, leads to the desire to create something better. Revolted against the world as it is, the disciple, in their imagination, starts to create an ideal world in which there is no suffering, neither human nor animal, there is no cruelty of nature that makes beings live at the expense of others. Feeding these strong thoughts, the disciple saturates the space with them and creates vibrations which are already actively protesting. Like this, passive on the physical plane, it becomes active on the astral plane.

The existence of these two binaries - one of the passive – active states and the other opposing disciple – Logos - characterises the second Arcana of the negative aspect of Swords.

In the 1st Arcanum - the Ace - of Swords, the disciple understood the illusory character of the physical world; in the 2nd Arcanum he understands that the astral world, that is, the world of structure or the world of forms that will later become manifest in the dense plane, also depends on a series of subjective and objective factors that condition such forms.

Having denied the reality of the physical world, the disciple now denies the reality of the astral world. In his consciousness a new binary is born: Relativity of astral forms - illusory character of the manifestation of these forms in the Earth.

Thus, in the second degree of Swords, the disciple lives the relativity of all "truths", of the affirmations of reason, of all "sanctuaries" and the paths that lead to them. He now knows that all of these are illusions that the human mentality creates, wanting to express the Inexpressible. He admits that other ways also seek to express the Truth, that there are "other sephirothic systems" and other "jacks", similar but different, serve the Logos with the same sincerity and dedication.

At this stage, the disciple's consciousness is centred in the "Nasham" plane (Manas, in the East) - the mental plane. It has not yet risen to the "The Haia" (Buddi) plane – the spiritual plane - and therefore the disciple is not qualified either to perceive the deep and common source of diverse worlds, or to make the superior synthesis. He sees the Universe in separate fragments, devoid of coordination and harmony and even contradictory. Consequently, he rejects the astral world - Yesod - as he rejected the manifested world - Malkuth. The collapse around him deepens.

In order to move forward, the disciple needs to resolve binaries, that is, by finding a solution that neutralises them. This will correspond to a new internal state and will constitute the passage to the next Arcana, the third.

3 OF SWORDS

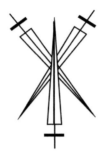

SEFIRA HOD – PEACE

The image shows a three-dimensional figure, composed of three swords: Two of them horizontal, which intersect with a vertical with the tip directed upwards and constituting a common axis of the other two, around which they revolve in opposite directions.
One of the swords symbolises the Logos and rotates clockwise, that is, clockwise involutive, because the force of the Logos descends from the most subtle planes for the denser ones. Another horizontal sword rotates in a contrary sense - the evolutionary - and represents the disciple which, despite its struggle with Logos, seeks to rise from the dense to the subtle. The third sword is the conscience which neutralises, in the ascending direction, the binary: Disciple - Logos. Each sword symbol has, along its full length, a channel that, as has already been said, symbolises the direct, potential connection between the physical and the spiritual.
During the 3rd degree of Swords, little by little, in the disciple's conscience, the understanding that the Creative Force of the world, against which she is fighting, is the expression of Something Higher still, as it is also seen that both Logos and she, the disciple, are

both reflections of a higher Principle. This awareness is the first step towards peace and future union with Logos.

At the same time, the disciple sees that, in her struggle against Logos, she seems to substitute Him, stopping alternately, from active to passive and vice versa. The imagery of the disciple is active in the astral plane, that of the Logos, in the physical. This exchange is represented in the image by the movement of swords, turning successively from one side to the other, from passive to active.

The disciple realises that, wanting to free herself from the illusions of the physical plane, she created new ones on the astral plane, and that the struggle with Logos itself is also an illusion. She understands that the relative character of the physical and astral worlds is a conception that arises in one's own conscience, due to conditioning, limitation and criticism of one's own mentality. So she understands that the binary, that reflects her reaction to the physical and astral worlds, is created by herself, by her own "mind". She also notes that the basic source of all his illusions, the cause of the struggle, the dominant factor in her revolt, is one's own intellectual principle.

From the point of view of the disciple's internal experience, this understanding is symbolised by the vertical sword, which neutralises both sides.

During the 3rd degree, the disciple gradually frees herself or himself of the illusions they created, which allows them to rise to the next degree.

However, in spite of its apparent uselessness, the struggle was necessary and indispensable for something that the same spirit could not understand. It relates to the experience of Sefira Hod, Sefira of the depths which gives birth to a more real life. During the passing of the first degrees of Swords, the disciple took leave of this real life, which is to the extent that the personal "I" is extinguished and where peace reigns forever. Now she/he knows how illusory this "I" is.

One of the aspects of Sefira Hod is expressed by a Law that has something that is inevitable. Driven by this Law, the disciple who has just learned from these illusions concerning the physical and astral planes, is subject to higher, metaphysical illusions, because it is during the 3 of Swords stage that she enters into what Tradition calls "the spider web of the Logos", which encompasses the field of influence of the four Sefiroth surrounding Tiphareth. That is, Hod, Netzach, Geburah and Gedulah.

4 OF SWORDS

SEFIRA NETZACH – VICTORY

The drawing that symbolises this Arcanum features a square, formed by four swords with pointed tips in an involutive sense. It is the symbol of something closed, limited by a current without end. The four arms - the crosses of the elements - take the place of the four Sephiroth, which constitutes the "logos spider web", of the Sephirothic Tree. It is the field of the creation of illusions.

These four Sephiroth condition, by their content, the realisation of the central Sefira, Tiphareth - the Harmony – whose place, for the time being, is marked by a single point, because the disciple, who is still fighting the Logos, sees only chaos, reigning on all sides. To himself at the Archetype level, there is nothing absolute. All is relative, unstable, changing; is the "panther" of Greek philosophy. He has not yet come to realise the superior harmony which penetrates the worlds. He got stuck in the "spider web", sees causes as targets, results conditioning the laws. Everything is mixed. The conception of time – an aspect of our conscience and a factor that helps to discern the cause of the effect - became nebulous.

The 4th degree of Swords is a turning point for the spiritual future of the disciple, not only with regard to the present incarnation, but for the next and even for a whole series of incarnations, because it is in this degree that one is faced with the desperate spectacle of the Universal Wheel, and born within him is a great compassion for everything that exists, or an animosity towards those responsible. The importance of these two possibilities is that compassion will become an inner Light, a Fire from the heart that will allow you to rise from the mental plane - Manas or Nesham - to the spiritual plane, Buddi or Haia. Animosity, on the contrary, will not only prevent you from overcoming the internal void you are experiencing, but will stimulate your fall, your involution.

The "spider web of the Logos" is the **PROVING GROUND** that every disciple needs to cross victoriously. Sefira Hod was the first step, the first awareness the disciple has of the illusory character of his struggle with the Logos, but also the internal need to continue.

In Sefira Netzach, a disciple is required to be self-determined, a purely ethical issue of his character. In this Sefira, the first reaction of the disciple to the world of the Great Illusion that revealed itself before him, proceeds. According to his own nature, it will prevail in him, or the spiritual impulse to sympathise with the closed world inside the square of illusions and crushed by its weight, or, himself, falling under the influence of various inferior emotions, irritability and malevolence, will be subjected to the weight of that square and his spiritual will and aspiration will become deformed. At this stage, the disciple needs to choose clearly between "spiritus dominat formam", or, that is, the victory of the spirit over the form - the traditional title which corresponds to Sefira Netzach - and "dominat form spiritum ".

This choice will depend on the future content of the core of the "spider web", that is to say, the degree of realisation of the Sephira Tiphareth on the Tree of Life. Only the internal force, the symbolic "axis", can help you to get out of this "spider web".

The life story of Prince Siddharta, the future Buddha, illustrates this victory well. Crossing Swords on one level, very high, the young prince feels such a great compassion before the spectacle of earthly suffering, which unfolds before him, that he abandons everything to help those who suffer.

Another example, however opposite, is that of Ivan Karamazoff, by Dostoyevsky. He is also strongly moved by the sufferings from which not even innocent children escape. Your reaction, however, is purely mental: It condemns the higher injustice. It is not the compassion that is born within him, the rebellion against that allows this.

5 OF SWORDS

SEFIRA TIPHARETH - HARMONY

The image of this Arcanum features four swords, with the handles located at four different angles and the ends directed to the centre. A fifth sword, perpendicular to the first four, points to the same centre and symbolises the radiant Spiritual Light that, from above, allows the disciple of this degree begin to better discern the Truth. This Light is the influence of the "Children of God", the Herald of Bliss, Superior Protectors, or, using the language of Ethical Hermeticism, the Initiates of Cups and Wands. These beings, sacrificing themselves for the general good, descend to the Earth and placing themselves in the centre of the "spider web of the Logos", create of themselves the Tiphareth of the world. Such sacrifice allows other beings to find their own "axis of the Logos", their Tiphareth, that is, their own and unique individual direction of ascending.
There are variations in the way and the form of the teaching of these Sent from Above. The Truth, Unlimited and Inexpressible for His Essence, can be presented only in one or another of its aspects, in one or another way that limits it. However, the form of the form is not essential; it is essential that these Beings exist, of that

eternal Ray of Light that penetrates the "spider web" and brings with it Divine Harmony.

The disciple, seeing a glimpse of this Light, is happy in knowing that it exists in other planes, but finds that it does not penetrate to the basis of the manifested world, that this still remains in evil. The disciple does not believe that anything can transform the world. He admits that this Light, perhaps, could help those who follow the precepts of the exoteric religions, who could sustain his faith, but in the faith that could help him, a disciple of the Swords who became more individual and independent.

He feels that nothing coming from outside can satisfy him, that Light and Harmony must be born within the self, that he, himself, must become a source of Light.

At that stage, the disciple who went through the trials of the first four degrees of Swords and stepped onto the fifth, approaches Tiphareth, but is still unable to perform this Sefira. To do it would be, for him, to overcome the opposites of his life, freeing the self from the illusions that led him to internal and external struggle; would mean creating within the self a new focus of consciousness that would dismantle the "spider web" that is surrounding him, and that would allow it to become its own "axis".

This is not yet the case. The disciple's trials ended. Harmony cannot be born within him and it crosses the central point of your Tree of Life, that is, the still empty place of Sefira Tiphareth, without realising it.

Nevertheless, the approach to the centre causes large changes, a new internal sublimation. If not in the past, the experience lived in the fifth Arcanum of the Swords would not be a new thing accomplished during the spiritual ascent.

Conscious of the Light and Harmony of those who reached the higher planes, the disciple feels, in an even more acute sense, his own loneliness and imperfection. He knows nobody and nothing can help him but himself. If even now it was fed hope, even unconscious, of some help, it no longer exists; it was definitely gone. Continuing his path, if he wins in the new trials, the disciple will return to the place of Tiphareth and create this Sefira with his own spiritual wealth, which he is acquiring for the sake of success.

The Woman with the Cobweb by Caspar David Friedrich

6 OF SWORDS

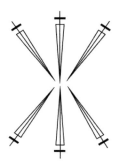

SEFIRA GEBURAH - SEVERITY

The picture features six swords with tips pointed to a common centre where there is nothing. That is, they are pointing to emptiness, non-being. The disciple voluntarily moved away from the salutary ray of the Sons of God, rejected all help, all direction, whatever it might be. Nothing else is sought and nothing expected. At this stage it seems your life has no more search or purpose, everything is nothing more than emptiness and against that there is no remedy.

The 6th degree is one of the most painful stages of Swords; it is a trial by the void, created by the disciple themselves. If he/she fails to overcome this terrible trial, their evolution will be interrupted. Within and around the disciple the void is total. He/she lives within a complete spiritual doldrums. There is no more revolt in them, the fight against the Logos is over, because they understood that both their person and their struggle were part of the plan of the Logos; that they were just a puppet on the world stage and only played a role that had been assigned to them. Therefore, he/she renounces any activity, finding it totally useless.

The disciple knows that their struggle for a better world and fight against the Logos were illusory, but they cannot return because, for them, personal will is no longer an impulse enough to get back to activity. The danger of this stage is precisely the cessation of any movement, even involutive. The energy that propelled the disciple towards a specific target, disappeared now for the absence of that target. **It is the crisis of greatest magnitude**, since for a long time all the will of the disciple was concentrated on the continuous spiritual elevation.

This stage corresponds to the rejection of Sefira Geburah, Sephira of Severity and the vital indispensable and justly established processes. In this state, the disciple does not perceive the wisdom of this "severity", but only sees the conflict of contradictory strengths. Such a state naturally leads to the loss of any interest in life and even the loss of any vital impulse. It leads to the desire to end it all and often results in a "philosophical" suicide. In the world literature there are many examples of such cases.

The experience of the internal void, in the negative aspect of Swords, can be lived on different levels. Each disciple of Swords has already experienced the "forbidden fruit "of Gnostic self-knowledge, which is not another thing like internal liberation. He can't go back anymore to the conditioned forms of Coins and their illusory "realities", because he has definitely passed them. Their tragedy consists in the rejection of all points of support in the physical and astral planes, that is, to have denied the "Kingdom" and the "Form" and also rejected superior aid, without having found it, in itself, the "saviour", the "axis of the Logos". Entangled in the metaphysical maze, the disciple wanders without "points of support" in a lower region and without any "suspension point" in the spiritual world. Only the inner state can help one to overcome this challenge and to perceive a new reality.

7 OF SWORDS

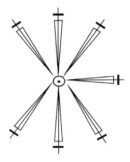

SEFIRA GEDULAH - MERCY

The image shows the same six sides of swords as the previous Arcanum, however, each one bears the symbol of a planet. In the centre, previously empty, we now see the symbol of the Sun, or Logos, which corresponds to the 7th sword, the perpendicular, looking from a higher dimension.

The seven swords represent the Seven Secondary Causes of our solar system, that is, the vibrations of the seven planets or the seven Rays of the Logos. In the picture, Logos seems to identify with the Sun, uniting the vibrations of the other planets.

The three "solar" planets, those in whose symbols figure the Sun, that is, Mars, Mercury and Venus, are placed on top of the card and the three "lunar" planets, with the Moon symbol, Saturn, Moon and Jupiter, are below. The disciple who managed to pass victoriously through the terrible ordeal of emptiness now faces a new test. The danger of this degree consists in that the disciple can govern these influences as independent strengths from one another, not completely synthesised by the "Sol" the Logos.

Just as it happened during the Coins internship, again he feels in himself the influence of the seven planetary forces and bipolarity (the separation of planets into solar and lunar). In other words, he finds himself in the real presence of the elements of the personality that, until now, he thought he had overcome.

The danger of this degree consists in the disciple being able to govern these influences as independent strengths from one another, not completely synthesised by the "Sun" or Logos.

Only through awareness, of its oneness with the Logos, will the disciple be able to unify the components of his personality with his conscience and simultaneously eliminate the self-affirmation of the lower self.

If this unification of the personality is not achieved, each one of the elements that compose it will remain independent and will have a divergent and separating tendency, which leads inevitably to the personality breakdown. If the disciple does not succeed in realising the "axis of Logos", that is, the 7th sword, or the synthesis of his personality, he will therefore depart from the six planetary rays that, by the cosmic Law are polarisations of the Sunlight or the Force of Logic. It will also make it impossible to synthesise the elements "M" and "F". It will become entangled in the sevenfold internal planetary chaos and the contradictions of the androgyne. The 7th sword will remain for him a "dead sun".

Until now, the disciple's process of subtlety, that is, of the disillusionment in the lower personal elements, was carried out consecutively under the strong influence of the negative aspects of just one of the planets.

Thus, the influence of the Moon (1st grade, Malkuth) was as if by the devaluation and negation of external "realities"; that of Mercury (Yesod, 2nd degree), for the rejection of the world of astral structure or forms; that of Saturn (Hod, 3rd degree), by negating the value of the rational and critical principle; that of Jupiter (Netzach, 4th degree), for the negation of the power of the unifier and illuminator of the Upper Light; that of Mars (Geburah, 6th degree), by contesting the value and refusing all internal impulses; that of Venus (Gedulah, 7th degree that we are studying), by negating the possibility of harmonious synthesis of the perfected elements of the personality.

In the 7th Degree Arcanum the disciple faces the last trial of the Seventh Plane Secondary Causes and failure, in that step, can lead to personality breakdown, for negative influences from all planets act to that degree with a renewed strength.

Overcoming this problem means transforming centrifugal and centripetal planetary strengths, separating into unifiers, creating a new centre in itself. The realisation of that Sefira, that of Mercy, undoes the "spider web" and allows the return to the Sefira Tiphareth – the Sefira of the Logos - and centre of the Sephirothic system.

However, the place that this Tiphareth will occupy, the new synthetic Sun, will not be the same as that of the ancient Tiphareth. This new Tiphareth will be at the intersection of paths 3 and 9, neutralising the Sephiroth Geburah and Gedulah, not in the sense of descent, as before, but at the same level as the two Sephiroth. In Hermetic Philosophy this point is called 'DAATH' or "application point of the Great Arcanum of Swords ".

The 7th sword, from above, represents the Logical synthesis and, in the sephirotic system, it corresponds to the Daath point which, in turn, symbolises "Reintegration", that is, the future restoration of the true esoteric, human nature.

Swords, as we know, is the suit of the Logos and therefore an androgynous suit. On the initiatic path, symbolised by the Minor Arcana system, it is in this suit that appears for the first time, as the reflection of the Superior and Absolute Synthesis; however, the Primordial Divine Source, still does not manifest. Progressing on his last trial of the planetary kingdom, the disciple becomes aware of his oneness with the

Logos and again becomes sevenfold and androgynous, but already in a way that is superior and spiritualised. Aware that his "I" is not separate from the Logos, the disciple, one might say, put himself in El's place. So planetary vibrations, until now external, become internal also. He lives, within himself, the interplay of the planetary forces, perceives in himself the sevenfold network of causes and effects. Realises that he is a reflection of an Inaccessible Reality, in his own conscience, that the activity of the Logos in the world, as he imagined it and against which he was fighting, was just an illusory conception created by himself. Now the discipline understands that everything has its existence in Logos, that all the planets are one with El, just like he, the disciple. Then the Path opens again before him. He recognises its uniqueness with Logos and the "axis of the Logos" itself, that is, recognises the Spiritual Principle in everything that he did.

That understanding becomes a Light that begins to reveal to you the wisdom that permeates the world. This will allow you to pass the "Nesham" plane (or Manas) to the "The Haia" (or Buddi) plan.

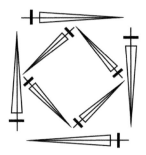

SEFIRA BINAH - REASON

In the image of this Arcanum we see two squares, symbols of the form; one is inside the other and each one is formed by four swords.

The external square, supported on one side, represents stability and firmness. It is the symbol of the יהוה quaternary law in the cosmic nature of Logos. The internal square rests on one of its angles, giving the impression of instability, insecurity and changes. It is a reflection of the same Quaternary Law in the soul of a disciple.

In the previous degree - the 7th - the disciple surpassed the influence field of the Seven Secondary Causes and became conscious of its oneness with the Logos - the Creative Power of the world. She feels herself the action of the יהוה Law and yet, inside it there is still a protest against the "Reason" that rules the Universe, symbolised by Sefira Binah and the divine name "Iave", which corresponds to this Sefira.

In the preceding degrees, being under the influence of negative aspects of the planets or, to be more exact, of the tatwas "coloured" by the planets, the disciple freed herself from some illusions, only to fall into others.

Rising from Sefira Geburah to Sefira Binah, the disciple entered the field of influence of the three upper Sephiroth. Now, despite her identification with the Logos, and perhaps because of it, the disciple comes under the direct action of the tatwas and, first, under its negative aspects. These destroy not only the illusions created by the disciple, but also any imperfection of its substantial nature and its personality.

We know from the study of the 8th degree of Coins that the four lower tatwas - the substantial ones - correspond to the quaternary composition of the human person. Let us remember the tatwas' relationship with the four elements that make up the manifested world. Each element is the most dense manifestation of the tatwa, to which it corresponds. Let's see how these tatwas-elements can act about the disciple.

Tatwa Tejas - which corresponds to the element Fire - in the negative aspect destroys everything, externally and internally; as positive strength, directed inward, it is a purifying factor. In the disciple, it purifies whatever is left of the personality, feeding its aspiration to the Superior.

Tatwa Vayu - Air element - corresponds to activity, to movement. As the negative, it strikes and separates; directed inward, as force; the positive instigates the activity of the soul, leading it to seek the Light, still unknown.

Tatwa Apas - Water element - is linked to adaptation, receptivity. On the negative side it rejects all forms, externally and internally; as constructive force, replaces obsolete or inappropriate forms with others, new and more appropriate.

Tatwa Prithivi - Earth element - corresponds to density, stability. On the negative side there is a need to lose "points of support", both externally, on the physical plane, as well as inwardly. Its constructive strengths help to find the "suspension points" in the upper planes.

These tatwas – which are strong - could transmit the creative impulse of the Akasha tatwa, but if the human being is not spiritually mature for direct reception (rather than through the planets) of the creative emanations of Akasha, or if there is disharmony in the lower tatwas that make it up, Akasha's action will be destructive or produce a distorted manifestation-science.

On the initiatic path of the negative aspect of Swords, the destructive action of the tatwas plays a very important role. In the early degrees of Swords, the influence of tatwas, felt outwardly, through the planets, manifested already as an impulse to destroy existing forms, an impulse, however, caused by the desire to create new and better ones.

In relation to a disciple, the action of the tatwas never expresses itself as a primitive vandalism or a proliferation of purely personal and uncontrolled desires, nor in a moral relationship or a psychological state in which every human being finds that everything is allowed, as happens in the case of people with little spiritual development.

When a certain level of evolution is reached, the destroyer influence of the tatwas goes inward, against the very imperfections and can even cause total collapse in one or another aspect of the human being. Usually, the higher the plane touched by the destructive action, the more severe its effect will be. So, on the physical plane a serious decrease in vital strengths may occur (perhaps caused by exaggerated asceticism); in the astral and mental planes this action may cause the mortification of the soul, devastation of the mind and even spiritual desolation, with the total loss of will and ability to live.

In the previous degrees of Swords, the influence of the tatwa Akasha, "tatwa of the abyss", acting on the disciple through the planets, caused the process of progressive dissolution of the lower elements of the personality, taking him (in the 6th degree) through probation by emptiness. After the disciple's unification with the "axis of the Logos", Akasha's action becomes direct.

In the 8ᵗʰ degree of Swords, the disciple disavows not only the illusions of the psyche and conscience, but also the whole personality, not because it is considered illusory, but because it is one of the ways of creativity of the Logos. The disciple, at this stage, although she feels included in the macrocosm, does not accept the visible world, created according to the יהוה Law, as she considers this Law as something external and opposed to her own aspirations.

That complicated psychological state is illustrated in the symbolic image of the Arcanum by the involutive sense - that of creation - the outer square, while in its own microcosm - the internal square - the direction indicated by swords is evolutionary, that is, it contributes to subtlety, the disciple feels that the tatwas of the larger square are hostile. Once again the desire for destruction is reborn and, if the disciple cannot find within itself a sufficient internal strengths to overcome the emotional element, that is, this desire for destruction, instead of sublimating their own personality it will become destructive, both externally and internally, entangling in the karma of the world. You may need to start over the way, employing even several incarnations to reach the point already reached. This is Tatwa Akasha's first negative, straight action. However, any destructive impulse that the disciple experiences in this Arcanum is not caused, as before, by despair or revolt, but because of the need to break free, open a path to something higher than she already has to sense. The essence of this process is the internal need for sublimation, that is, of the evolutionary movement, opposite to that of creation.

This drive for liberation can take two directions: the exoteric, leading to destruction, and the esoteric, leading to sublimation. The path of destruction leads to a new void, still deeper than the 6ᵗʰ grade test.

The sublimation path, on the contrary, constitutes an indispensable preparation for a new and superior life of the soul. It is your liberation from everything that is dense, that weighs down and prevents elevation. So, the square of the Logos, in the symbolic image of the Arcanum, solid and stable, no longer seems hostile to the disciple. She now knows that the destructive impulse that she experienced and that turned into internal subtlety, is an integral process of the Laws of Logos, and that the desire to free oneself from imperfect forms, illusions and the crystallisation of the material world, is also an aspect of these Laws.

Having overcome the danger of failure on her spiritual way, the disciple finds that the destructive action of tatwas helped her to definitely overcome the personal element in herself. It includes the reason and value of the process for each step.

A new, positive phase is taking place for the disciple, still in the same Arcanum; her personal content was sublimated by positive action of the tatwas.

She becomes receptive to the superior and creative aspect of Akasha that allows you to transform yourself progressively, to form a "cup", emptied and ready to receive new spiritual content. She now sees that the very void that so much made her suffer, helped in the formation of that cup.

She is no longer the disciple who wants the sublimation of the world, but she attains her own internal realisation, thanks to her merger with the Logos.

The dissolution of the imperfect personal elements unleashes "the human creator" and the creative energy comes to fruition over the Primordial Source. The human being and the Logos liberate each other.

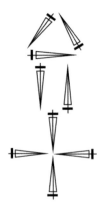

SEFIRA CHOKMAH - WISDOM

The image corresponding to this Arcana presents nine swords forming three separate groups. On top, three swords form an ascending triangle, which must be imagined spinning in the evolutionary direction. Sword tips are directed in the same direction. In the centre – two vertical swords: the one on the right with the tip directed to the top; the one on the left - down. At the bottom, four swords, with the points directed towards a common centre, forming a cross. It is the traditional pantacle of Initiation, adapted to the suit of Swords.

We know that the basic idea of this pantacle - the Initiation on the three planes - always remains the same. However, each type of Initiation has its particularities and details of the general pantacle of the Great Arcana of Initiation, can change too. The 9th Arcanum of Swords underlines the esoteric nature of this suit and its Initiation.

The relationship between the pantacle and the יהוה Law remains also the same. The top triangle corresponds always to Iod-He; the centre symbol, be it a hexagram or some other representation of the binary, corresponds to Vau; the bottom symbol, which can be a square, a cross or a cross within a circle, corresponds to the second He. The pantacle can also symbolise the Initiatives of all four suits of the Minor Arcana. In that case the lower part represents the Coins Initiation; the centre, that of Swords, and the superior one, the Initiations of Cups and of Wands that, as already mentioned, are internally linked and complete each other.

The suit of Swords has a binary character. This one expressed, first of all, by the two ways of crossing the suit: The philosophical or negative (rising from Malkuth to Keter) and that of the faith or mystic (descending from Keter to Malkuth). In the symbolic image of the Arcana, the two modes are represented by the two swords in opposite directions.

If we analyse the pantacle exclusively in relation to the negative aspect of Swords, the binary character of the suit will express itself through two possibilities of crossing each degree: That of destruction and that of sublimation.

We must not forget that the central part of the Initiation, your "Vau", also always indicates the mode in which the initiation process takes place. The opposite directions of the two swords symbolises the fight. On the negative path of Swords, the disciple fights the creative power of the world - the Logos. On the positive side, the struggle is against its own elements with the intention of creating a more perfect personality.

Let us analyse the pantacle only from the point of view of the suit of Swords. At the bottom, the cross formed by four swords is the יהוה Law which forms the basis of the experience of each suit. In Coins, it was the "four Mage's toys" or, also, the four elements. In Swords, it is the cross of the tatwas that "destroy and are destroyed and that build and are built". These four tatwas manifest, in the lower planes, the influence of the 5th tatwa, the Akasha which, descending, creates the other four. The superior tatwa, Akasha, although invisible, is present, "crucified" in the centre of the cross, pointed at by four swords.

In the middle part of the pantacle, the two swords, in addition to symbolising the struggle, also indicate the means of progress. The sword with the tip directed downwards (the descent through the Sephiroth) symbolises the path of faith (the positive) and the struggle against your own imperfections. The sword with the tip upwards (uphill from Malkuth to Keter) represents the philosophical (or negative) path, revolt and struggle against the Logos and the progressive dissolution of the lower elements of personality. Finally the top triangle, rotating in an evolutionary direction, unlike the immovable triangle of Coins, symbolises the movement and changes of mental elements. In conclusion, due to the experiences lived in previous degrees, the state of consciousness of the disciple changes. The old way of thinking disappears, leaving another in its place. The disciple experiences a kind of disintegration of his mental and astral bodies, as if he no longer possessed the ability to think and feel. The characteristics of three-dimensional life (for example: past, present and future, and those related to them, such as Karma, Providence and Will) often merge. The laws of logic - thesis, antithesis and synthesis - no longer have the same vigour. The relationship between cause and effect is not so clear as before. The way of thinking, which was logical and rational, it becomes more irrational and intuitive. The disciple no longer identifies with the circumstances of his material, astral or mental life, that is, with what constitutes the human personality. Inevitably, this causes a sensation of internal emptiness.

In the last degrees of Swords, it is not only the psycho-mental state of the disciple which changes, but also their self-awareness, which in a personal way is supra-personal, that is, it rises to the level of Haia (Budi in the Eastern nomenclature). This purely rational experience is felt as an annihilation of the self and can be fully understood only by someone who went through it. Every personal element becomes extra for the disciple. Personality in itself is still considered useful, only to the extent that it performs a necessary function in the world of the "non-I". In this process all the personal dies, so that supra-personal can be impersonal. That's why Tradition calls the Initiation of Swords "Initiation of Death".

The "reality" of the personality, so important for the vast majority of people and even for a disciple who reached the Coins Initiation, fades away. The personality becomes illusory. But, every genuine initiatory process is a process of birth of something new, of a new spiritual being. The Initiation corresponds to the descent of the Higher Force, as a result of the internal transformations and the sustained effort by the disciple to rise. It is a meeting of two forces: The upper and the lower.

The spiritual level of the Sword Initiation is, of course, higher than that of Coins; the disciple became more subtle and more tight. However, we underline, once again, that the Initiation of Swords, as with each esoteric initiation, is not an isolated event, but the result of a process that, as the case may be, can be longer or shorter, a spiritual development process. The Spiritual Principle, in essence, is always the same, but the way to contact this varies to infinity.

So in Coins, for example, the action of the Spiritual Principle manifests in the disciple for his work of organising and harmonising the personality, of "building your Hierophant's Cross". Now, at the Swords stage, as the personal elements disappear, the manifestations of the Spiritual Principle can be more direct, as the Force no longer needs to go through the prism of personality, even if harmonious, but only for individuality. The Arcanum of the Sword Initiation corresponds to Sefira of Wisdom, Chokmah. Wisdom, at the Swords stage, manifests itself by understanding the illusory character of the World of Coins, both external and internal; for awareness of the very relative value of all personal accomplishments and magic and understanding that the only reality is the Spirit.

In the preceding degree, that of the Sefira Binah, the disciple passing through it on his own, before being considered "reasonable", achieved the achievements achieved. In spite of the fact that Sefira Chokmah is freed from itself, that is, from that which, then, she considered to be "I" and, reaching a superior wisdom, she would like to know her supra-personal existence.

In the story of Jesus' life, we find many episodes that can serve as examples for different suits. As "Son of Man", Jesus had the experience of all grades and suits, living them up to the highest level. So, He had mastery over the elements, He could chase away demons and perform other miracles. He established a chain made up of twelve disciples and confirmed the Law and the Prophets, all of which are part of the Coins suit. Your prayer about the cup and His acceptance of the destiny that expected ("Your Will be done") are characteristic of the Cups suit. The foundation of His Church is a mission belonging to the suit of Wands.

However, it seems to us that the human nature of Jesus manifested itself with greater strength in the experiences of the type of Swords. The agony of Gethsemane, the "Via Crucis" and Crucifixion are the most intense examples of experiences of the suit of Swords. On the cross, Jesus seems to lose His divine character. If it were not so, His sacrifice would not have been complete.

It is important to underline that in all these manifestations and spiritual states of Jesus there was no established sequence of suits or degrees, as it happens in the life of a disciple, because Jesus was already a God-man, following the path of Reintegration. Jesus was crucified on the cross of matter, cross of the elements, of the manifested world. It is a very high living symbol of the human spirit, nailed to its material envelope, on the cross of the lower tatwas. As a human

being, Jesus passes on the cross a terrible moment of
solitude, of total internal desolation. "My God, my God,
why did you abandon me?" It is a real fusion with the
suit of Swords. Soon after, the cry "I am thirsty", with
which Jesus, as Son of Man ", passes again to Cups.
In the Golgotha episode we find yet another symbol of
the great Arcanum of Swords: The two thieves, that is,
the two swords directed in opposite directions. One of
the thieves did not know how to overcome the "trial of
death", he became insensitive to the Superior attraction.
From the inner void, he goes back to the beginning of
Coins, demanding tangible evidence to accept the Divine
("If you are the Christ, save yourself and us"). The other
has faith in the divinity of Jesus, he aspires to
redemption or, in symbolism of the Minor Arcana, the
passage to Cups.

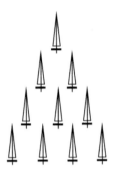

SEFIRA KETER – CROWN - RADIATION

In the drawing we see a pyramid composed of ten vertical swords with the ends pointing upwards. This presentation indicates a certain similarity of all the elements that compose it.

There is no more whirlwind created by the encounter of the tatwas in the centre of the cross, there is no bipolarity in the depths of consciousness, that is, nothing else exists of what constituted the essence of the initiation process. Now, everything is polarised in one direction: Upwards.

In the 9th grade, everything was still in motion, as the degree included and synthesised the initiation process of Swords, that is, the dissolution of personal elements on all levels. In the 10th degree you have stabilised your aspiration for the High.

The base of the pyramid consists of four swords that symbolise the tatwas-elements. The swords are the same and point in the same direction. This means that all planes of the new personality are harmonious and totally sublimated.

In other words, it means that the letter gradations of the יהוה quaternary law merged into only one aspiration to the High and that the need of the previous sequence of the creative process ceased to exist for the disciple - initiate. The sublimated personality (the four swords) is now a solid base on which all transformations can take place internally within the disciple.

The three swords, immediately above the four, symbolise all ternaries. Sublimation or "esotericisation" of consciousness makes the ternaries merge harmoniously in one reality only. So, for example, the division of time in the past, present and future, so logical and clear to ordinary human beings, fades progressively, replaced by the irrational concept of the "eternal present", in which, according to Revelation, "there is no more time.".

Similarly, the elements of the mystical triangle - will-karma-providence - begin to merge, little by little, in a single totality, because among these principles which, until then, determined human life, was eliminated any antagonism or struggle; they mutually complete and condition.

The swords placed on top of them also must be opposed, because in the new consciousness of the disciple all the binaries are united in a superior synthesis. Thus, the cause and effect, good and evil, active and the passive principle, "M" and "F", etc., are no longer opposed or diverge, they are all polarised in the same direction: The High. The laws of logic and reason lose their value and their reality, because the last illusion of the mental body - the thought that created images and shapes – also now fades.

We don't forget that the thinking process is an attempt to express everything in words, that is, to give everything a mental form and find a relationship between the forms thus created. Now, the disciple's thinking becomes more and more intuitive and contemplative.

The last sword, the one above, represents the disciple. It is the symbol that expresses the meaning of your life, now entirely directed upwards.

The 9th Arcanum of Swords pantacle presented the scheme of the internal transformations that characterised the initiation process of Swords. The pantacle of the 10th Arcanum presents the new state of composition of the personality of the disciple, to which these internal transitions led him/her. This new state can be briefly characterised by the full sublimation of all the elements that compose it.

the 10th Arcanum of each suit is the final result of the total initiatic process of the suit. In Coins was the realisation "non-I" and the use in the environment of everything that had been reached.

In spite of the fact that, due to the negative aspect of the Swords, the disciple does not do anything externally in search of something. Their achievements are purely internal. This stage consists, first of all, in the transformation of the internal content, from which the lower "I", inferior to the personal, is completely excluded.

The conscience of the initiated disciple of Swords no longer identifies with that little "me", in the relationship with his or her environment, neither does the disciple intend or seeks to change anything in anyone. His internal realisation does not manifest itself in anybody's contact with the world around him, due to the total absence of his "small I", his personal interests and own wishes

She seeks solitude. Solitude in general helps internal development; in addition, the disciple becomes too different from his peers, who continue to live inside their "little self". It is through the criterion of this "I", of this mirror that everything is deformed, that people receive external impressions and react to them. The disciple, on the contrary, rejects this "I" as something despicable and fleeting.

Most men seek earthly happiness. The initiated disciple
has already experienced the impassable happiness of
internal spiritual experiences and therefore no earthly
happiness is capable of attracting him/her. In the
external world, he lives like the "Fool" of the 21st Major
Arcanum, embodying the "Shin" principle, in its higher
esoteric aspect. He will feel different, even from the
people who are his dearest ones, and also feels that he
is not yet able to share his Light with others and,
consequently, the world.

The internal preparation that gives the ability to
transmit the Light to others constitutes one of the steps
through the Cups, whilst awareness and the real
experience of the true "I", besides any form, already
belongs to the suit of Cups. It is the "Crown" reached
after the painful path of Swords; the "Radiation" of the
transcendental world that will become internal and
constitute the permanent "suspension point" for the
initiated disciple.

The Keter of the Swords is the threshold of a new state
of consciousness, because the Initiation of the Swords
has transformed the initiated disciple into a "container"
or "Cup" which, however, is still not full and, therefore,
in the process, sharing your content with others.

*****

As already stated, the negative aspect of Swords, like
the 'steps of all other suits, can be traversed at different
levels and aspects. However, if several people cross the
same suit, at the same level and under the same aspect,
their experiences will be similar, but not identical.

In the current presentation we gave just one general
and typical example of the negative path of Swords, but
the way of living your experiences and their sequence
can vary a lot, because spiritual life is deeply individual,
unique and unrepeatable for each human being.

There are, however, general characteristics of this stage. These are, for example, the devaluation of personal realities, both external and internal, acute awareness of the illusory character of life in the world and the relativity of all "truths" and human affections, sensitivity, profound suffering and suffering in the world, the complete internal loneliness and desolation and, finally, the disappearance of the personal "I" and the appearance of the internal Light.

What has just been said about individual character of the Swords experience also refers - and even more so - to the top two suits: Cups and Wands. We will outline online one characteristic example. The way where the soul goes through these suits is deeply individual.

CUPS

The experience lived in the Cup suit is completely
different from that lived in Coins and Swords, that is, it
differs from everything that, until now, has been crossed
on the way of the initiate.
In Cups there is not even the continuous scourge to
progress, in order to always acquire more knowledge
and hidden powers, which characterised Coins, nor the

ardent search and hopelessness of the
inaccessible Truth, the internal
struggles, the scepticism and martyrdom
experienced in Swords.
We repeat, again, that the negative stage
of Swords has nothing to do with
nihilism, atheism or some type of soul saturation, or
else, with deep immersion in materialism. The move to
the suit of Swords was made possible by the sincere
search for the immutable values of life, and the
direction that this experience took was determined by
the internal search for the Absolute Truth, a search so
total and fiery than all shapes and shells, which
envelope Truth, were rejected as successors unworthy of
Her, like man-made idols, like lies that misrepresent it.
Only when the Swords disciple reaches the ultimate
limits of their mental, astral and physical endurance, do
they begin their merger with the Transcendental Truth.
So, it opens like a flower to the light, it becomes a "cup"
to receive the Divine Light.
The symbol of Cups, the full cup overflowing, represents
spiritual maturity. The essence of the Cup suit is not
just internal spiritual life but is also the receipt of the
gifts from Above and their transmission to the world
that surrounds the disciple-initiate.
The Cup stage is not a "path", that is, it is not a
sequence of internal and external obstacles, of
realisations and transformations, as was the case of
Coins or Swords, but a progressive sublimation of its

receptivity, a "widening" and "deepening" of your "bowl",
so that it can receive as much of the Light as possible
and thus also give more to those who need it.
In the Sephirothic system there is a downwards passage
through the Cups stages - from Keter to Malkuth - for
the disciple receives from above and transmits
downwards.

ACE OF CUPS

SEFIRA KETER - CROWN, RADIATION
Traditional title: "Existencia"

The image of the Arcanum presents a cup that must be imagined as full. It cannot be empty, as it is the receptacle of the Divine Light that, filling it in the last degrees of Swords, determined the passage of the initiated disciple of Swords to the suit of Cups.

The law of Cups is the law of Transcendental Life, the law of Primordial Light permeating the Universe, of the Holy Spirit, of the Mother of the World.

For a World Cup disciple, the whole world presents itself as an immense "cup", prepared to receive the Divine Light and needing It. The disciple himself, too, is prepared to accept with gratitude everything that comes from above. This acceptance, however, is different from that of Coins. Now he knows that everything is good, everything is necessary, everything has a higher purpose. No one and nothing will be destroyed, because everything is sacred, everything is part of the Divine Life, of the Family of God.

This internal state provides the disciple with a great harmony. His "Cup" overflows with Peace and Light and he yearns to be able to transmit them to other beings, because now he realises there are thirsty "cups" everywhere. He therefore returns to the external world, to teach, heal, comfort; to continue living in that world, however, considering himself just a receptacle, a channel to transmit to others the Divine Force. That is the expansion of Cups.

Lived in its superior aspect, the suit experience of Cups, corresponds to the "state of sanctity" of the religious conception. This experience can sometimes manifest itself as the ecstasy that is known to Catholic mystics and is a state of exaltation, accompanied by gestures and exclamations; it can also manifest itself by enstasy (the opposite of ecstasy), consisting of deep withdrawal into itself. The latter is closer to the orthodox egregore and also to the eastern "samadhi". Enstasy is characterised by complete immobility and the experience that is being lived can be perceived only by sight.

Traditionally, "Cups are placed on the stems of Swords" (fig. 12). This means that only after having crossed the stage of spiritual growth of Swords does the disciple acquire the ability to open up or, symbolically, become a "cup" for the genuine Spiritual Light and transmit it to others.

Figure 12

He who has not yet burned his personal elements, who did not go through the purifying sufferings and the trials of Swords, is not yet able to serve as a "cup" for the Truth, because in the passive state, receptivity is necessary, his conscience does not rise fully and automatically to the higher spiritual plane – the plane of Truth - but remains open to mixed influences and, at times, involutive manifestations of the various astral planes; he is impressed with the lying charms of the planes, taking everything as true revelations. All Christian saints speak of these dangers. H. P. Blavatsky also mentions them in her little book, "Voice of Silence".

These are "false cups" and the overflow of their content can cause great damage, spreading false teachings, creating false teachers and false prophets, as a consequence of "false sanctity".

SEFLRA CHOKMAH - WISDOM
Traditional title: "Unicity"

The image shows two standing cups, one next to
another. Above them - a Caduceus. One of the cups
symbolises the Teacher, that is, the disciple-initiate of
the Swords who has now returned to the world to teach;
the other is the student. These beings, aspiring to the
same objective target, are attuned and harmonised,
resembling the coiled serpents wrapped around the
Caduceus rod. The student's full cup means he has
received as much as he could assimilate.
The more light the Teacher transmits to the student, the
more he/she fills their own cup, because the cup of
ONE, overflowing, fills the Master's bowl again. It is
communion between two units.
Through their individual reaction to the Truth received
from the Master, the student unconsciously enriches
the Master, because for this it is very important to know
how the student reacted to the Truth, what aspects
were assimilated and how they have transformed their
consciousness.
Studying the student's individual reaction, the Master
discovers new aspects of the Truth, which makes their
own awareness wider and deeper. So, the greater the

circle of students, the greater the enrichment of consciousness of the Master, because his own Light adds to Light from others.

This communion between the Master and the students is possible only because the Light that everyone receives is the same. The difference is only in the reaction that takes place. This is an important aspect of UNICITY, which characterises the present Arcanum.

The Master's cup was the first to open to the Light and he receives it directly; the student receives through an influx from the Master, but the Source of Light is the same; therefore, the Light received by the student, although transmitted, is genuine.

There is, however, a case where the student can also receive the Light directly: It is when Master and student, mystically united, are, therefore, "side by side" under the illuminating light of the Caduceus.

It is possible that the student has reached only the internship of Coins, or even, that he/she is still on the path of initiation and has not yet harmonised his personality. Even so, being "side by side" with their Master, at the moment of receiving the Higher influx, the student rises, symbolically speaking, "through the central column of the Sephirothic system" to the plane that corresponds to the metaphysical essence of the suit of Cups.

It is necessary to underline the difference that exists between an initiated Coins instructor and a Master of Cups. It influences the fact that the former is due to the prestige of his own personality, his authority. It's the "magister dixit[6]". A Coins Initiate can give the student a little bit of their magic power, experience and knowledge, or enable them to be a part of their own conscience and realising power or to make the same as a gift. Naturally, in this case, it is not possible to speak in equal terms, nor return to the instructor what was received by the student. Here, the student partially

---

[6] "the teacher has said it"

reflects the instructor and, for the student, the instructor is the only source of Light, strength and knowledge that is accessible.

A Cup Master gives nothing of himself, but only transmits what he receives from the Superior and his authority consists of the great reverence felt before that Superior Force.

It should be noted that a human being who reached the stage of Cups, therefore, becomes a "Master or Cup Initiate". In the Russian Orthodox egregore he is called "Starets[7]", in India, "Guru", in the mystical orders of dervishes "She" and in other branches of the spiritual path, by other names yet.

Cups is the suit of Bliss, of the laws that govern receptivity to the Superior emanations, of adaptation and transmission of the received. The first Law of this suit is that the Master's "cup" always remains full, as he may also receive from all students everything that is in their "cup", which is always from the Superior. The nature of Cups creates a very special relationship between the Master and his student.

All men, as children of God, are equal. It is the basic human equality. But there is also another type of equality: Esoteric equality before the Spirit, when both Master and student receive directly the same Ray of Light. However, as a personality, they naturally cannot be the same, because in this case there would be no "Master" and "all is ONE".

The "Cup student" is a conditional term, given to each one who seeks the Light of these "Men of God". A "student" can be an ordinary person, already sensitive and attracted by the magnetic streak of the Master. Remaining a certain time in his aura, he takes with him a fragment of his Light, and in this sense, become his disciple. However, there are also true disciples, in the

---

[7] A spiritual director or religious teacher in the Eastern Orthodox Church, or who is not necessarily a priest but is recognised for his piety and is turned to by monks or laymen for spiritual guidance.

occult-esoteric sense of the word. They are the ones who chose and follow this Master permanently.

As an example of such followers, we can mention Motovilov, in relation to Seraphim Sarov; Aliosha, in relation to Zósima; Vivekananda, in relation to Ramakrishna In such cases, the time between the teacher and the disciple is formed by a great love and the Master's prayer can realise between them oneness of the Spirit.

THREE OF CUPS

SEFIRA BINAH - REASON
Traditional title: "Infinity"

The image shows a cup placed on top of the other, forming an ascending triangle. This Arcanum is a reflection, in relation to the colour of the Cups, of the Sefira Binah, Sefira of Universal Reason, which transmits a low-level impulse that comes from Keter. The Sefira Chokmah, the first one to receive this impulse, was transformed, in the Cups, in an individual form - a cup - both of the Maestro and of the student. The second degree of the Cups was related to the donor unit and the recipient, that is, the teacher and the student, both receiving from the Fountain of Light. The third Arcanum says about the Fountain, symbolised in the third cup, which could be considered as neutralisation, in the ascending direction, of the binary: Teacher - student.

This is the dynamic cycle יהוה in the process of the initiation of the Cups. Light in the Teacher's cup (י Iod) and in the cup of the student (ה He) passes from one cup to the other and, in the blending, a new cup (ו Vau) is created, predominating over the other and, at the same time, feeding them. It is the realisation of a new unit (the second He), which is a new step in the way of the Initiation of the Cups.

All the egregores and all the worlds in the life of the One and the three of Cups, in reality, symbolises the Living Water of the Divine Bliss that composes its waves. For the disciple of this degree, the Universe is the manifestation of the One Life. The Oriental esotericist expresses that Brahma, Vishnu and Shiva are not separated, but are three Aspects of the Divine One. In the states of Cups or Swords, they were perceived as separate or as consecutive states. In the state of the World Cups, they are merging, solving the problem of the terrestrial concept of Good and Evil, of their relativity.

The Infinite is the merger of Good and Evil, as relative concepts, and a sole manifestation of the One Life.

The title of the third Arcanum of Cups - Infinity - points to the ontological nature of the third cup, that is, the Incommensurability of the Divine Bliss which reveals itself as Transcendental Life - the Universal Mother - from which everything comes and to which everything returns.

The disciple who came to live this state has already overcome their karma and personal karmic responsibility. He/she does not judge anybody else, because they see only the cause and reason of each weakness. The only thing that is important to them is that the "cup" of the soul of the human being is able to receive a fragment of light, however small.

In the story of the life of Jesus, the fishermen, uneducated men, were sensitive to his words because, despite their imperfections, their "cups" were in a condition of being receptive to the Light, whilst the "cup" of Nicodemus - an astrally pure man and an ignored disciple of Jesus - remained closed until the resurrection of the teacher.

SEFIRA CHESED (GEDULAH) - COMPASSION
Traditional title: "Humility"

The image shows four Cups: Two standing at the bottom
and two placed above the first and facing down, as if
they mutually exchanged their content. It is the symbol
of the יהוה realisation process in the suit of Cups.
Separating the set formed by the cups, in the vertical
direction, we have a positive side (the right) and a
negative side (the left). The upper active cup symbolises
the Divine Flow. This fills the Master's cup (the upper
passive). The Master, in turn, transmits the Flow to the
student or students (bottom left cup), from which the
Flow goes to the lower right cup - the deposit of the
Light received by all who need it (the world cup). From
here, the Light rises again to the upper right cup.
It is the scheme of the eternal succession of the descent
and the ascent of the waves of Transcendental Life.
Relating to the four stages of the transcendental wave,
the cross of the elements or the four "hermetic animals",
we will have the following correspondences:

Upper right cup - element Air, Eagle;
Upper left cup - element Water, Man or Angel;
Lower left cup - element Earth, Bull;

Lower right - element Fire, Lion.

The predominance of one of the elements is expressed in the particular character of the work of a Master of Cups. The predominance of the Air element gives a certain quality of penetrating the influence of the Master in his environment. It is the same in the case of their physical absence, in that their presence is still being felt.

When the Master's influence goes beyond his environment and, indirectly, covers a more vast area, until reaching and perhaps even surpassing, the national egregore, whatever the predominant element of the Master, the simple fact of its existence, even after its terrestrial life, is felt as a mode of "omnipresence". It awakens in men the aspiration to reach the level of Master and, for that very reason, uplifts them spiritually.

In relation to people who are not in the initiatic way, but who achieved internal harmony, this is characteristic of the influence of the element Air in Cups, enabling one to feel in the environment the impression that "one breathes better". People who experience it often do not understand the cause of this sensation.

The Earth element is expressed by a greater connection with all the vital processes, within and on the Earth. In the Master of Cups, this is manifested by the accentuation of his sense of personal responsibility for everything that is happening in the world, for all the human imperfections that he strives to redeem, through his suffering, accepting and taking upon himself, even in an infinitesimal part, the karma in the world. This state makes him pray for the whole world.

The Water element is characterised by natural movement from top to bottom, from "Heaven" to Earth. In the Master of Cups, it is manifested by the desire to transmit to others what is received from on high. It is the acute awareness of being only a "Cup", the content of which must be given to those who need it. This transmission takes place through the direct contact with all those who wish to receive the Light from that Source. With the predominance of the Water element, the impulse to teach, to be a spiritual food, to heal all the evils of the soul and body of those who come to seek help, is expressed with a maximum force.

Fire is always in motion and always directed up. In the Cup suit it is the spiritual fire, the fire of the heart, which expresses itself in the intense love for God and for other beings, that is lived by the Master of Cups. The Master's love covers everything and everyone, those who deserve it and those who do not deserve it and that love doesn't need words or gestures to light a spark in the Cups of those who are in the field of its influence.

However, these four elements that in the Cups suit can express themselves more or less do not constitute different types of initiation. The Initiation of Cups is unique and all four aspects are present in it, that is, the influence of the Master acts through all four elements, although one or the other may manifest with greater strength, thus expressing the individual principle of the Master.

The 4th Arcanum of Cups is the reflection of Sefira Chesed (Gedulah), Sefira of Mercy and Compassion. It is the compassion that makes the Master of Cups return to the world to transmit this Light and the beneficial Strength he received, to spiritualise matter and subtlise the astral substance. He spills his "cup", offering the world all its content. He embraces the whole world and merges with it; it is the "Tat tvam asi" of the oriental mysteries.

The Master of Cups is inseparable from everything that goes on in the world. For him, everything is one. It is a fragment that contains everything in itself, like a drop of water contains in itself the characteristics of all the waters in the world.

This awareness gives rise to a great HUMILITY (title of the present Arcanum). The Master feels the evil of the world as present in itself, as if it encompassed universal karma. He considers himself infinitely distant from the perfection and unworthy of the Divine Light of El, which constantly aspires and that, however, always fills his/her "cup". This state experienced by the Master of Cups is the consequence of its deep connection and fusion with the world. Harm can no longer penetrate the world through them, because the Master's "cup" contains only the Water of life, of Eternal life.

The awareness of their imperfection and, consequently, contempt for their own person is typical of the state of holiness and would not be possible without great humility and the complete disappearance of every personal element

5 OF CUPS

SEFIRA GEBURAH - LEGALITY & SEVERITY
Traditional title: "Redemption "

The image shows five cups: Four are placed as in the previous Arcanum, forming a square and the fifth, in the centre, must be imagined as perpendicular to the other, belonging to a higher plane.

The fifth cup is the love of the Master of Cups, which leads to sacrifice for your environment and perhaps for all the world. It is, therefore, the Redemption cup. The content of this cup is a reflection of Transcendental Life and Transcendental Love, that is, the Redemptive Principle of Logos.

G.O.M., in his Encyclopaedia of the Occult (Tarot Majors), says that the Logos, in the Archetypal plane, "nourishes" with and transmits the Transcendental Influx, which is the Cosmic Love that, descending to Earth, makes life arise. Because of this, the fifth cup, in its superior aspect, symbolises also the Redeeming Blood of Christ, shed for the redemption of humanity. It is the Holy Grail of medieval legend.

A Master of Cups follows the path of Logos and resembles, himself, the Redemptive Cup of the Logos. However, in the symbolic image, the Cup of the Master of Cups stands up, oriented towards the meeting of the handles coming from on High, from Logos.

Sacrificial love, which now inspires the entire life of the Master of Cups, is not a common, emotional love. With the will of Logos, this love, in Sephirotic language, also expresses superiority of Legality and Severity.

The fifth cup of this Arcanum synthesises the possibilities and achievements of the four others, with regard to the transmission of Light to the world. It also synthesises the four aspects of the Initiatic Mission of Cups referred to in the preceding Arcanum, since all four are means of redemption, purification of the aura of the world and, therefore, of its spiritual evolution.

A Master of Cups does not renounce the world, he does not claim to be a God, but accepts himself as he is. He sacrifices himself for your wellbeing, taking a part of your karma. He knows there cannot only be "Son of God" but must also be "Son of Man".

The sacrificial cosmic love, which will open the redemption cup, is not only the expression of the Akasha tatwa, but also the upper tatwa - Anupadaka - acting through Akasha. This is Divine Love, which in the Eastern mystique is called "Talil".

The Akasha tatwa, whose influence is sometimes felt already at the Coins stage, is an expression of spirituality; the Anupadaka tatwa corresponds to a higher spirituality, that begins to manifest itself in the World Cup and Wands stages.

The 5th Arcanum of Cups is related to the 5th principle – the individuality - which allows the Master of Cups to receive the transmission of the Superior Force. The role this process plays in the individuality is underlined by the fact that the fifth cup is on a higher plane.

In the kabbalistic interpretation, this cup corresponds to the letter "Shin" placed in the centre of the יהוה cross. Like this, the 5th Arcanum is a reflection, on the plane of Cups, of the cliché of the Redeemer, יהשוה or Iehoshua. The "Encyclopaedia 'of the Occult" by G.O.M. explains widely the meaning of this kabbalistic name, which is the formula which determines the characteristics of each living organism that is:

1) Birth of a similar being (Iod);
2) Growth (He);
3) Nutrition (Shin);
4) Procreation (Vau);
5) Death or passing to another plane (second He).

In relation to the Cup suit, the formula "Iehoshua" corresponds to Transcendental Life, transmitted to the world by the Cup Master. The "Shin" element of this formula is the individuality of the Master, whose manifestation depends on the degree of their conscience and their realising power, which, in turn, are interdependent. These factors depend on what the Master is able to receive from Above, the plan he receives and is able to transmit to the world. The "Shin", in this formula also corresponds to "nutrition", only now spiritual rather than physical.

6 OF CUPS

SEFIRA TIPHARETH - HARMONIA
Traditional titles: "Patience" and "Hope"

Patience is the characteristic of this Arcanum, its "modus operandi ". But patience would be unimaginable without hope of reaching reach a final target. The Apostle Paul says that from patience comes experience and from experience, hope.

The Arcanum image features six cups. Four are placed as in the previous Arcanum and symbolise the same. The fifth cup, standing, is above the two superiors and forms with them an ascending triangle. The sixth cup, below the bottom two, faces down to form a descending triangle with them. The two triangles are not interlaced and therefore do not form a hexagram. The upper cup receives the Divine Light, the bottom collects terrestrial suffering. The upper one transmits the Light received through the two cups below it. The bottom elevates suffering through the two cups above it. The upper cup corresponds to the Son of God, the lower to the Son of Man.

Seen on the cosmic scale, the symbolism of the 6th Arcanum, completing that of the 4th Arcanum, corresponds to the descendant and ascendant flows of Transcendental Life. A Master of Cups unites these

Flows, in him or herself. Like this, he joins the suffering of the world and elevates it. The symbol of this process is Christ on the Cross, uniting in Himself the earthly suffering and the Divine Light and changing, with that, the aura of the Earth.

So that the substance of the world, on all levels, can be changed, the two cups must merge into the soul of the Initiate. Not even the bottom cup, despite all the terrestrial agony, nor the upper bowl, despite the abundance of Divine Light, separately can realise it. Note that nothing spiritualises the person as much as suffering, whether physical or moral, especially when accepted with patience and serenity.

The great saint of Cups, Francis of Assisi, says we cannot boast of the gifts of God, for they are not ours, but are received from God, but we can boast of the cross of our sufferings and afflictions, for these are ours. Suffering plays an important role in the life of all the saints. It is probably necessary, not just as payment for past karma, but also as a purifying and spiritualising element, which helps in the formation of the "cup".

The 6th Arcanum is the central Arcanum of Cups, the reflection of Tiphareth, Sefira of Beauty and Harmony. It is the harmony between the Divine and the Human, between spiritual happiness and terrestrial suffering, through Patience and Hope.

7 OF CUPS

SEFIRA NETZACH - VICTORY
Traditional title: "Resurrection"

The image shows seven cups, of which six form two independent triangles, that is to say, they are not interlaced. A bottom triangle is of the descending type and the cups that form it are standing upright. In the upper triangle, of the ascending type, the cups are turned down. The seventh, standing, is in the centre and must be imagined as belonging to a higher plane. The ascending triangle denotes the continuous aspiration of the Master of Cups, the Divine Light. This comes forth abundantly and then the cups are turned, spilling it. A descending triangle symbolises the Master's return to the world, to transmit the received Light and raise it (the cups are standing).
the 7th Arcanum is the result of the process carried out on the 5th and 6th. It is an internal disorder of the human being, caused by the deep penetration of the spirit in the matter and the transubstantiation of that matter in spirit. The seventh cup symbolises this process.

One of the Initiate's tasks is to elevate to a higher plane the substance of their physical body. The most exalted symbol of that realisation is the Resurrection of Jesus. In the Resurrection, a superior state of matter was manifested, proving that Jesus had changed the tactical composition of His physical body, moving from the dense state to a full dematerialisation of the elements that made it up.

A Master of Cups, zealously following the path of the Logos, makes the process of transmuting the effective substance of their physical body. However, consciously collaborating in carrying out this process, he never does it with the intention to acquire supra-physical powers or for some other personal purpose, but to spiritualise the general matter of the world.

An initiate from Coins aspired to immortality but wanted it only for himself. A Master of Cups sacrifices himself to the immortality of the world. An initiate who succeeds, even if only partially, in transmuting the substance of their body, performs, with that action, something for the whole world: It makes subtle the lower planes. It is a step forward in the general evolution of the world, a step that not only shows the way for other beings, but also makes it easier in the future.

The spiritualisation of matter is another aspect of the "resurrection of the dead", that is, of inactive forces inside the man. It is his release from the yoke of matter, the yoke that limits man's spiritual possibilities and makes it difficult for you to know yourself and the world that surrounds you.

The subtle use of the physical and etheric body takes place by the opening of the psychic centres that, at this spiritual level, are naturally and involuntarily made as a consequence of general spiritualisation, as a gift from Heaven and not due to the lower plane activity. The ability to "think with the heart" and to "feel with the mind" also helps in this process.

As an example of such a transformation of the human being, he can serve the "Righteous" of all religions, whose open centres enable us to manifest various hidden powers, such as clairvoyance, clairaudience, telepathy, psychometry, exteriorisation of the astral body, levitation, etc.

The 7th Arcanum closes a cycle. The Cup Master held complete internal harmony and the ultimate victory of the spiritual about the material. Because of this, the name given to this Arcanum is "Victory". The specific victory of Cups is by sacrifice and by patience in purifying sufferings. The seventh cup is the symbol of a new Harmony, the Harmony that is not only internal, but radiates its strength over the world that surrounds the Master of Cups.

The 7th Arcanum of each suit is related, in one way or the other, with the 7 Secondary Causes - the planetary insights reflected in the human being. In Coins, the planets influenced the work of purification, harmonisation and the disciple's personal achievements; in Swords, the type of trials and the ways of "dissolving" the personal elements. In Cups, the influence of the planets is revealed for the gifts of the Master of Cups and for his ability to serve the world. This relationship can be outlined as follows: The predominance of the Sun is expressed by personal magnetism, attracting to the Master even completely different people; of the moon, by the gift of reading human hearts and minds; in Mars, by the ability to ignite the purifying Fire in human Cups; in Mercury, by the ability to resolve with wisdom the most complicated human problems; in Jupiter, by the gift of spiritual authority; in Venus, by the force of love, emanating from the Master; in Saturn, by the power of prayer that can produce miracles.

8 OF CUPS

SEFIRA HOD - GLORY, PEACE
Traditional title: "Fraternity"

The image shows a chain forming a circle and composed of eight cups, placed in the evolutionary direction and which empty their contents, one into the other. It is the symbol of the great fraternity of souls that was established after their resurrection, that is, after the victory, in them, of the Spirit over Matter.

It is also the symbol of universal human fraternity as it exists in the consciousness of a Master of Cups. For him, there are no differences in race, religions, nationalities. All are brothers.

This awareness of universal fraternity, unknown to the great majority of men, determines their relationship with each human being. A similar fraternity can sometimes establish itself within a group, very united internally and where each considers himself a link in the chain, outside of which it would exist only as an isolated fragment.

For a Master of Cups there are no enemies (these are possible only when there is self-affirmation of the personality), not even strangers. For him, all men are truly "close", members of the same family, bearers of the Divine Light, present in each one.

The Master of Cups seems to perceive neither evil nor human failures. However, he sees in every human being a different form of "cup", all containing the Divine Essence, even if the owner himself still knows nothing of this.

For a Master of Cups, all imperfection comes from elements inferior and alien to true human nature. A Master of Cups does not judge anyone, because, due to Superior Light that illuminates him/her, they perceive an abyss of imperceptiveness in their own fleeting personality.

The 8th Arcanum of Cups is also the Arcanum of the formation of the egregore, esoterically objective. This, in a natural way, surrounds each Master of Cups who accomplished the inner spiritual victory and who overflows the Light of their "cup" into the "cups" of the disciples and of those who, being in tune with him/her, are receptive to his influence.

In the 2nd degree of this suit we speak of the existing union between the Master and the disciple and the exchange of Light between their "cups". The egregore is formed on the same basis as the exchange of Light. In the symbolic frame all the cups are equal and the Master's cup which created the egregore is not distinguished from others.

Whatever the Master's internal achievements, they belong to everyone, in the sense that each one, forming part of the chain, can use the Master's strength if necessary. Each link in the chain receives everything it is capable of receiving, making his/her particular experience an egregoric wealth common to all. The cups of the pantacle are connected to other connected ones. What belongs to one, belongs to others, as there is no longer a separation of personalities. The Master's personality seems to dissolve, remaining just a source of Light, common to all.

The esoteric current of Cups is created from the first link - the Master - who other souls approach, attracted as if by a spiritual magnet and, to this connection, the theurgical nature of the fraternity grants a Special meaning. The Master is the first to receive the Divine Light and his/her "cup", overflowing this Light, makes souls that tune in with it, as in a chain reaction, also become receptive to the Light. "Attract the Spirit of Peace", says the Seraphim of Sarov, and a thousand souls will be saved around you". There are no separate initiations here, neither degrees nor personalities. It is the union in the Spirit.

Often an "ashram" is formed in the place where a saint of Cups lives. Monasteries appear in the neighbourhood and many souls are transformed, even after the saint has left the physical plane.

The eight of Cups is a reflection of Sefira Hod. It is this Sefira that relates to overcoming the personal element, after the victory of the spiritual in the preceding Sefira. The Cup suit is not just about the total disappearance of the personal element so that Something Superior can be expressed, but also of the union, in the name of this "Something Superior" with all those who, in one way or another, live the same state of consciousness. This union is the "Glory" of victory over oneself and the "Peace" of an egregoric creation, internally solid.

SEFIRA YESOD - FORM, THRONE
Traditional titles: "Faith" and "Joy"

The image shows nine cups, in three groups: Above, three standing cups form an ascending triangle; in the middle are two standing cups and at the bottom, four cups go outwards from a common centre and form a cross. Here, as in every 9th Arcanum pantacle, we have a trinity, a binary and a quaternary.

The 9th Arcanum of Cups is truly your "Great Arcanum", as it is the complete synthesis of the achievements of other degrees and not just the accumulation of its results, as in Coins or Swords. The Arcana of the Cups suit do not represent certain steps on the ascent leading to the Initiation and the different ways in which the internal state of the Initiate is expressed. In Cups, your "cup" always becomes more open and deeper, that is, fuller of the Light that the Christian religion calls "gifts of the Spirit". The esoteric nature of the Cup stage is essentially different from that of Coins or Swords. Cups belongs to a superior suit, free of conditioning and limitations of self-awareness, that is, of consciousness directed inward. This was definitely overlapped. The internal disorders that were processed in the lower suits, due to the continued shifting of the focus of consciousness, are no longer present in Cups, because now that focus is established in the supra-personal. However, "self-awareness" is not to be confused with the "personal conscience" of a Master of Cups, that is, with his mental functions, conditioned by the time he lives on Earth, by the environment and other factors. "Self-awareness", as we said, is directed into the person himself; "personal conscience", on the contrary, is directed towards the external world and it depends on the degree of receptivity of the surrounding human beings. In this sense, even a Cups Initiate belongs to his time, being in contact with its ideas and with the religious concepts that are reflected in his personality and through which, many times, manifest the Spiritual Principle. So, taking this form through mental conditioning, this Principle, in turn, makes subtle the mental.

Pure spirituality, purely spiritual experiences, are never conditioned by time or space. Therefore, as a testimony of the Real Existence, the experiences of mystics of ancient times have the same ontological value as the mystics of more modern times.

The Cup stage is a state of sanctity and is, therefore, unlike the usual state of an ordinary human being or even a disciple. This must be taken into account to be able to understand and analyse the pantacle of the 9th Arcanum of Cups. This can no longer be divided, as in previous suits, into the partially mental, astral and physical, because these exceeded the limits of personality, entering the supra-personal field.

The crown of the Cup Initiation must be analysed under three aspects: The field of pure spirituality (upper ternary); the field of the spiritualised psyche or soul life (central force) and the field of the total personality of the Initiate. The upper ternary represents the spiritual essence of the Initiate, in its three aspects: Existence –

Knowledge - Bliss, or in the Eastern terminology: "Sat", "Chit", "Ananda". The "Existence" is the Real or Transcendental Life that flows through the Initiate. The birth for that life marked his passage to the World Cup suit and corresponds to the disappearance of definitive "self-awareness".

Real Life inevitably influences the other two aspects: Knowledge or Higher Gnosis and Bliss that now, as a result of contact with the waves of Real Life, permeates the whole being of the Initiate. It's the Oriental "Nirvana", truly and esoterically understood.

Note that Knowledge - positive or active pole of the ternary - acquires a relative form through the mental and helps you understand Real Life. Bliss - occupying the negative or passive pole - takes shape through feelings and allows you to feel Real Life. The three aspects coming together harmoniously bring the Initiate closer to the Absolute Truth.

The two cups in the middle part of the pantacle represent the Initiate, both in Spirit and Matter ("Purusha" and "Prakriti" in the East). For an Initiate of Cups, the Spirit permeates and spiritualises the whole Matter and is manifested by the Spirit. The two cups also symbolise the thought and feeling binary which, sublimated, are no longer separated. Within an Initiate of Cups, feeling and knowledge are inseparable; he "knows with the heart" and "feels with the mind".

The quaternary of cups at the bottom symbolises the subtlety of the whole personality. The lower four tatwas, perfected, symbolised by the cups, emanate from a widespread centre - the 5th tatwa, Akasha. On the physical plane, this is expressed by a natural asceticism, that is, a minimum of the matter, as a result of general spirituality.

It is the reduction of the need for sleep, food and other needs related to the physical body. On the etheric plane, there is an increase in personal magnetism which, due to its highly harmonious character, becomes curative (for example, cures by the laying on of hands). Hidden powers also automatically appear. In the field of feeling and thinking, as we just said, there is a complete harmony.

One of the most characteristic consequences of contact with Real Life and the disappearance of "self-awareness" is the feeling of nullity itself and, to a certain extent, contempt for yourself. It is interesting to note that this characteristic appears when the personality starts achieving a high degree of refinement and harmony. This apparent paradox is not difficult to understand. As the disciple progresses, he realises a horizon of other spiritual dimensions and, simultaneously, the insignificance and meanness of his own person. For an Initiate of Cups, aware of the splendour of the Spiritual World, the whole personal element totally loses its value. Furthermore, the Initiate never considers the transformation that he will carry out as his own merit, but as a proof of Divine Grace.

The lower quaternary can also be analysed as an expression of the יהוה Law, but at the level of creation. In the suit of Swords, the law of causes and effects, that is, of logical and inevitable sequence, began to lose its vigour and to appear as an illusion of the mind. Now the Master of Cups understands that the world exists due to the impulse of Higher Will that spontaneously manifests itself in each creative act and in the cause of the automatism of causes and perceptible effects in the human mind. You know that the world - the living organism of God-Logos - is created by the same Law, יהוה, but acting on a different plane, higher and mentally inaccessible.

The 9th Arcanum corresponds to Sefira Yesod, which has two traditional names: "Form" and "Throne". These are names, which, with respect to World Cups, point to another characteristic of this spiritual stage: The return to form.

In Coins, the form constituted the support point for internal work and development of the realising power. In Swords, the disciple rejected it as an illusion. In Cups, the Initiate goes back to it again, but only as a medium, differentiating himself from the disciple of Coins. The Master of Cups no longer needs the forms as support points for himself; he simply admits them as necessary for the evolution of humanity. The value of the form for the evolution of humanity, of the appropriate form which does not distort the essence, consists in that, without it, the Higher Truth would be totally inaccessible to the human mind. In this way, a Master of Cups, understanding the esoteric value of the form, accepts the external appearance of dogmas, rites, etc. Without losing forms, the Initiate would not be able to carry out his World Cup mission, to transmit the Light that fills your own "cup" and other "cups", for any "cup", even that of the Master, is a form.

The human soul, in a sense, is also a "form", a "throne" for God, because the soul keeps in itself and transforms in its inimitable way the Divine Light, Light which he received and which, by his nature, is beyond anyway. Tradition gives two titles to the 9th Arcanum of Cups: "Faith" and Joy". the first underlines the purely religious essence (Religion: Connection of man with God) of this spiritual stage. Indeed, in Coins reason prevailed; at the negative stage of Swords, the disciple was taken by the revolt and protest; the positive stage of the same suit, already it was happening under the influence of faith. However, only in cups does faith reach its full superior theurgical expression, for it becomes internal knowledge and the internal experience lived in Cups, in turn, confirms the faith.

As for the second title, "Joy", we mentioned in the chapter of Coins the specific joy that accompanies each disciple of Coins who works on the same and observes his progress. After the painful prongs of the Swords, the Initiate of Cups, who entered the Transcendental Light, experiences a much greater and more perfect joy, because its nature is already purely spiritual. This joy differs from the irrational and fleeting experience of enstasy or ecstasy and it is the continuous state of the

Cup Initiate. It is the happiness of knowing Real Life, of being able to transmit to others your internal Light, of perceiving in everything that exists, even in the greatest of sinners, Divine Beauty.

Parsifal revealing the Holy Grail, Franz Stassen

SEFIRA MALKUTH - KINGDOM
Traditional title: "Amor"

The image shows ten Wands, all standing, in four superimposed levels, forming a pyramid and corresponding, from top to bottom, to the numerical value 1, 2, 3, 4.

The 10th Arcanum of each suit is the Arcanum of Achievements, that is, of application, whether in the world of the "non-I" (as in Coins), the world of "I" (as in Swords), of everything that was accumulated or synthesised in the initiatory formula of the 9th Arcanum of the corresponding suit.

In the Cup suit there is also an achievement – the mission of Cups. This, however, is accomplished by the simple power of Love towards all that exists.

The upper cup of the pyramid is the symbol of Divine Love lived by the Cups Initiate. It is Love as a Cosmic Fountain, as Life and Creative Strength, because God is Love and where such a form of Love exists, the Divine Principle is present. The whole world comes from Love in its basic aspects: That of irradiation and of attraction.

The two cups on the next level represent God and the Man-Initiate. The Initiate is totally receptive to Divine Love and, in turn, returns that Love to God, through the manifested world - Malkuth, the "Kingdom" - because the Initiate of Cups returned to this world and remains in it, concentrating in itself all its vibrations and uniting them through Love.

Oriental mysticism speaks of two paths: "Bhakti" (the Love that leads to Knowledge) and "Jnana" (that of Knowledge that leads to Love). Ramakrishna, a great Initiate of Cups, almost contemporary, called his own path "Jnana-Bhakti", uniting them in One Cosmic Love. The following three cups symbolise the reflection, in the Initiate, of the Divine Trinity: Father - Mother - Son or Father – Holy Spirit - Son. The Three are, united by Love, inseparable, as one-existence. The love is Life inseparable. The Apostle John says: "We know that we pass from death to life, because we love our brothers" (the Epistle, 3:14).

In the Cup Initiate, Love-Attraction predominates, He fuses with the Mother, but knows the Father and follows the path of the Son, the Logos. In the Wands Initiate, as we will see more of ahead, the Father's Love-Irradiation prevails.

The entire evolutionary path of humanity takes place through the action of these two forces and, in this way, the Initiation of Cups-Wands already represents Realisation. In Cups, the wave of Transcendental Life (the Mother) elevates Sefira Malkuth (the World) to the Father, that is, the Kingdom of the Spirit.

The bottom four cups symbolise the action of יהוה in Cups. It is the Law of Love in the world. The Iod is Love that fills the Master's "cup"; the first He is the overflow of that Love to the other "cups"; Vau is the action of that Love within the "cups" that receive it; and the second He is the formation of a chain, whose links are united by the Love-Attraction that flows to them through the "cup" of the Master.

Tradition considers that the 9th and 10th Arcana of Cups already belong to Wands. This means that these Arcana anticipate complete passage to Wands and that, due to certain characteristics, belong to both suits. These characteristics are:

1. The 9th Arcanum is related to the Internal Light Source, present in a Cup Initiate. Without being a Source of Light, he could not pass to the suit of Wands.
2. The 9th Arcanum concerns the use of form, as a means of expressing a Truth, inaccessible by its essence. The Wands initiatic mission consists precisely in finding a suitable way to make understandable the teaching or religion that the Initiate wants to broadcast.
3. The 10th Arcanum is the Initiate's Love for all that exists. Without this higher Love, the mission of Wands would be impossible because it requires a total sacrifice for life itself, for the spiritual good of others.
Let us not forget that the Initiations of these two suits are, in the reality, a single Inception, with Cups being its passive receptive pole and Wands, the creative active pole. It is interesting to mention that this connection, in one aspect very low, in cartomancy, was expressed by a rule according to which the Queen of Cups, who represents the synthesis of this suit, is considered the "lady of the heart" of the King of Wands, which in turn represents the synthesis of this suit itself.

WANDS

In Hermetic Philosophy, as has already been said, the study of each suit of the Minor Arcana always follows the "diabatic" path, that is, descending, from subtle to dense, from Ace (Keter) to 10 (Malkuth). In Ethical Hermetism or the initiatic path - object of the present study - the diabetic direction does not always correspond to the experience lived by the disciple.

The Coins stage was the realisation and manifestation of human possibilities and their consequent application in the world of "realities". In Cups, the Initiate transmitted, downwards, the Spiritual Light received from the Superior. In these two suits, therefore, the way was the descent.

In Swords and Wands, both directions exist. In Swords, the path of faith, or the positive, also follows the "diabatic" direction, but the philosophical or negative path is "anabatic", because it is sublimation, starting in "realities" from the dense plane (10 or Malkuth) and, through struggle and suffering, raising the "Radiation" of Keter (the Ace). This path could be called internal reforming of the "sword" in the "cup".

The specific characteristic of Wands is that, in this suit, the "diabatec" and "anabatic" directions are being followed simultaneously and correspond, respectively, to the objective and subjective aspects of the suit. The goal is to carry out the mission of the Initiate in the world and corresponds, therefore, to the descent. At the same time, the Initiate follows subjectively the "anabatic" direction, of the most sublime "dissolution", leading to final Reintegration.

Progress in these two opposite directions is closely connected to each other. More complete and perfect is the objective realisation of the Initiate's mission in the external world, but in his subjective ascent, he approaches closer to God; and, the higher he or she rises on its individual climb, the more successful will be their mission on Earth.

A Wands Initiate does not create new worlds, like that which makes the Logos but, on our planet, introduces and shapes new spiritual values, new teaching and new religious movements. Their influence is not limited to their environment like that of a Coins Initiate but it achieves a vast number of souls, beyond the limits of their country and their race, and creates values that remain for centuries.

Your work is to give a new form to the Eternal and only Truth, when the old ways no longer meet the needs of human beings or when it the time comes to reveal a new aspect of Truth, which until then has been hidden. The reason for your mission is Love and you should be ready to sacrifice everything for the spiritual good of humanity.

This is the objective aspect of the Wands suit. The subjective aspect corresponds to simultaneous, internal experience. What does it consist of?

If we make an approximation between the complete path of the Minor Arcana and the internal composition of the human being, we could consider the Coins stage as a process of an initiatory process for the personality, that is, of the psycho-mental aspect. In this stage, the development of the Ruach - Nasham principles (Kama Rupa or Lower Manas, in the East), comes to its peak and the first glimpses of The Haia (Manas Superior), are a stimulus for the work.

The Initiation of Swords is, in reality, that of these same principles, caused by a deep internal crisis. The mental body, becoming receptive to influence from "The Haia", totally changes. As a result, the Ehida (Buddi) principle, takes the disciple to the stage of Cups.

The only initiation of Cups and Wands relates to the higher planes of the human being. In its Cup aspect it allows the initiate to live the state of enstasy or ecstasy (Samadhi); in Wands - the Initiate reaches the level of the "Divine Self" (Atman).

Wands is the suit of higher spiritual activity. In the first place, thanks to the suit, the Initiate is transcendentally connected with the Higher Spiritual Principle, still as something external; in the last three degrees of the suit, which in the sephirothic system belong to the World of Emanation, this Principle, for the Initiate, becomes immanent, therefore, in this upper stage of Wands, the process takes place with the Primordial Source of Light, Life and Love. Individualised consciousness changes, because it dissolves in any form, including the "cup". This is, in summary, the general idea of the subjective path of Wands.

With the Wands stage, experienced at its highest level, ends the spiritual climb of a human being on Earth.

It is worth remembering, however, that in all suits there are several levels, symbolised by the figures of each suit. Keeping the specific character of their suit, these diverse levels lead to the realisation of various spiritual states. At the highest level, Wands leads to final Reintegration. We know that the four suits match the sacred letters יהוה which, in turn, symbolise the Divine Principles of the "First Family".

At the level of the Divine Archetype, the Father (Iod) – Active and Creative Love - is inseparable from from the Mother (He) - Attractive Love, manifesting itself as Transcendental Life - because the First Aspect is only manifested by impulse towards the Second. Similarly, in the Minor Arcana, the Wands are inseparable from Cups, as only through the "cup" can the Wands fully transmit the Divine Influx to the world.

In the Hermetic Philosophy, the highest suit, Wands, corresponds to "Iod". In Ethical Hermeticism, that is, the ascension through the initiatic path, Wands correspond to the Second He, in which, as we have just said, the human spiritual climb ends in the holy land. The 9th Arcanum of Cups is that of Joy or Spiritual Happiness; the 10th - that of transcendental Cosmic Love - is reflected by the Initiate as the "thing itself", as "numinous". Due to these characteristics, the last two

Arcana of Cups already belong to Wands. However, between the Love of Cups and of Wands there is a certain difference. In Cups, Love is passive. The Initiate receives it from on high, experiences and radiates it. Love in Wands is active and creative to the world.

The changeover to the Cups suit takes place when an Initiate of Swords leaves his isolation because he feels able to share the Light he has with others. The passage to Wands takes place when the Master of Cups becomes aware of his internal Spiritual Force and receives a calling to carry out a terrestrial mission. From his passage to Wands, the Initiate gathers in himself the realisations of the two aspects of the unique initiation of the two suits.

ACE OF WANDS

SEPHIROTH KETER AND MALKUTH
Traditional title: "Creativity"

The image shows a wand directed below and in which you can see the traces of four cut branches that follow a spiral line. It's the same wand that the Wizard holds in his raised arm on the card of the 1st Major Arcanum. The raised wand symbolises the potential strength and the four cut branches represent the יהוה Law, which means that, one day, when the wand is lowered, it will express its realisation and this force would manifest itself in the external world.

The presence of this internal strength is the condition of power, which, metaphysically speaking, can be defined as the capacity to unite the multiple in one, to unify everything that was separate. In other words, the unity is the basis of the principle of power.

The symbol of the Wands – the wand-stick - is very widespread in the world. We find it, first of all, in magic. The Mage's "wand" is, until now, a walnut stick (with four cut branches), as the walnut absorbs, guards and better transmits astral fluids, in this case the fluids of the Magician, whose power commands the astral entities.

We also find the "wand" in the form of the staff of the pastor and the spiritual pastor, the Bishop. We find it as the sceptre of the king, the staff of the marshal and the master of ceremonies, baton of the orchestra conductor, etc. In all these cases it is the symbol of the power to maintain a particular order, unity or harmony. The magician's rod that is lifted on the card of the 1st Major Arcanum, however, has a dual symbolism. In addition to the strength, also shown is the Height as a source of this strength, which is confirmed by the sign of infinity, above the wizard's head. This double symbolism is reflected in the two simultaneous movements, in opposite directions, in the suit of Wands. The Ace of Wands includes in itself the two initial moments of the Wands stage: The initiate's awareness of his internal strength, leading him to start his mission, and the powerful impulse of will to reach fusion with the Primordial Light.

The one wand facing downwards, in the symbolic image of the Arcanum, represents the Initiate's first creative impulse, as a reflection in his or her soul of the active, creative Love of the Logos.

The creation of the World by the Logos includes processes of differentiation, of multiplications of the manifestations of life, if it could be decided to "disseminate" the One in the Multiple. Each part of this Multiple - the biggest sage or the smallest pet - has its value, its raison d'être and its place in the world, and the Logos once again joins the Multiple in the One. Wands symbolises the initiate's descent to participate in this unifying work from the Logos.

The Wands Initiate modifies the existing forms of life, giving them a new essence and simultaneously destroying everything that has become obsolete in them, everything that has lost its reason for being, becoming just an appearance, an illusion. He does not "put new wine in the old wineskins", because "wineskins" are also renewed.

The Wands Initiate knows the reason and why of each way, he clearly sees the essence of everything and therefore has the right to destroy deceptive appearances, "Maya". He also knows that his strength comes from above and that the more you grow individually, the more you can give of your world.

2 OF WANDS

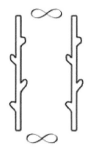

SEPHIROTH CCHOKMAH YESOD
Traditional title: "Salvation"

The image features two wands, side by side. The one on the right is pointing downward, the one on the left, upwards. Above and below the two wands is the sign of infinity.

In the two processes of differentiation and integration, in all planes of existence, from the infinitely small to the infinitely large, from the infinite above to the infinite below and vice versa, regardless of the point where the movement starts, everything is permeated by the Divine Principle, which is the same in all planes.

Therefore, it can be said that evolution, in the absolute sense, does not exist, because it does not encompass intrinsic existence, but covers only what was distinguished by the Logos, that is, the manifest. Evolution is the passing of inferior forms to superior ones in life and, therefore, is linked to concepts of multiplicity, perfection, space and time, because evolution is the return of Differentiation to noumenal Oneness, the manifestation of forms of the existence of the "thing itself".

On the cosmic plane, the two wands in the image symbolise the work of Logos: That of creation (the descent) and that of sublimation (the climb). The Wands Initiate voluntarily takes a certain part of the latter, so he can work only for evolution, that is, sublimation. Participation in the cosmic creative work of the Logos is not accessible. The descending wand, therefore, in relation to the initiated, symbolises his own descent into the world.

In the first degree of the Wands suit, the Initiate was aware of the Impulse of Divine Love. Now, this Love is invested with Wisdom, because the mission must be carried out not only with "Love", but also with Wisdom. The 2nd degree of Wands corresponds to Sefira Chokmah, Sefira of Divine Wisdom. According to the teaching of Hermetic Philosophy, the field of this Sefira was the "place" of permanence for human souls before the fall, that is, in the "Institutio" stage. In relation to Wands, Chokmah corresponds to the Influx of Divine Wisdom and its expansion in the soul of the Initiate. The Initiate's Wisdom, of its mission on Earth, must consist, first of all, in knowing clearly which element would need to be introduced into the spiritual life and which must be destroyed. The lack of this insight would result in failure of its mission.

The Initiate frees himself in this Arcanum in all ways of consciousness through which karma is created. In other words, the achievement of this degree corresponds to the overcoming of personal karma, with all the consequences of that internal initiation act. However, whilst freeing himself completely of the forms, the 2nd Arcanum of Wands, which also corresponds to Sefira Yesod, simultaneously links the Initiate to new creation and ever more perfect ways for the evolution of humanity.

The two realisations - the objective and the subjective – explain the traditional title of the Arcanum: "Salvation", In fact, objectively, the Initiate's mission is to save human souls from the second death, the esoteric, in which the soul separates itself definitively from the Spiritual Principle. The ever-increasing depravity of the soul can lead it to that final decomposition. Saving oneself means keeping the "eternal memory", that is, immortal consciousness.

The Initiate's mission also includes helping souls to overcome negative karma in their own right, as well as the general negative karma of humanity. Subjectively, the "Salvation", of the Initiate consists of the merger with the Divine or the "Atman". In the East, this corresponds to a passage to Paranirvana; in the West - returning to the home of the Father.

The released Initiate could, if he wanted, incarnate again on Earth to do some work, but the general karma of the human being no longer has power over him.

The concept of "Salvation" is linked to the esoteric teaching about the redeemer cliché יהשוה or Iehoshua, what Tradition calls the "descent of the Christ" or, according to Eliphas Levi, "help from the Saviour". Remember what was said about the cross of the elements that compose the human being and correspond to the sacred letters יהוה. The central point, which unites the four arms of the cross, corresponds to the letter Shin, the "quintessence" or Superior Principle that governs the four other components, thus symbolising the total human being.

Another symbol of man is a straight pentagram in which the upper tip (Shin) or essence, predominates over the four substantial tips. The inverted pentagram, on the contrary, symbolises the predominance of substance over essence, that is, involution. However, this interpretation is not always correct, because, seen from the Archetype plane, the inverted pentagram symbolises the descent into the manifested world of the Spiritual Principle.

The letter Shin, in the centre of the cross of the elements, symbolises the Divine Word or Logos, "nailed" to that cross, that is, in matter. Likewise, the inverted pentagram can symbolise the descent of the Spiritual

Principle, the Logos, and the Christ's mission through the Man-Jesus. This pentagram - the Saviour cliché - is one of the most powerful symbolic protectors in Magic. Each Wands Initiate identifies, to some degree, with the saving mission of the Logos, as it descends into the world to help the evolution. Its symbol, therefore, can also be the inverted pentagram, resembling the "Hanged Man" of the card of the 12th Major Arcana, which gives the world the Coins of your spirit.

Wands, being the suit of missions, always corresponds to the initiate's descent. Simultaneously with his/her descent is their propensity to ascend and return to the Father's House.

3 OF WANDS

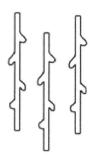

BINAH AND HOD SEPHIROTH
Traditional title: "Sacrifice"

The image shows three vertical wands that are aimed
downwards, next to each other. The level of the middle
wand is lower than the other two, so that the ends of
the three wands form a triangle of the descending type.
Binah is the Sefira of Reason. In the direction of
descent, it manifests itself as limiting the Divine Influx
of Love, already involved in Wisdom.
This means that in their mission, the Initiate has the
possibility of transmitting to the world only a limited
expression of the Divine Influx received; this therefore
means that he/she must measure and limit its spiritual
potential and realising power, adapting it to human
receptivity and the concrete conditions of time and the
environment in which it operates. All external work of
the Initiate is conditioned by these factors.
As for its internal state, this corresponds to the base of
the inverted triangle, the base that is above and in
which absolute peace reigns, the peace of Sefira Hod.
The sacrifice of the Initiate consists precisely in
renouncing the peace of Sefira Hod, renouncing
immersion in the peace of the inner spiritual world, in
order to return to activity in the lower planes.

This renunciation would be necessary for the Initiate to be able to continue his individual spiritual climb; it really seems that the very fact of renouncing makes possible the passage to a higher degree.

The importance of this waiver is that, being an absolutely free decision, it is not a "sacrifice" required by the circumstances, but a spontaneous and voluntary act, expressing an internal state. The words of Jesus: "... I want mercy and not sacrifice ..." (Mat. 9 / 13) has a profound esoteric meaning.

A sacrifice that has its root in the animosity of the environment, such as, for example, martyrdom for an idea fought or unpopular, provokes a karmic reaction, influence in the karma of the world and carries the karma of those responsible for what happened.

The spontaneous and "sacrifice-mercy" in which the happiness of being able to do so predominates over suffering does not turn the karmic wheel; but instead, creates a wave of harmony. Such a sacrifice, despite being often overlooked by the environment, and perhaps justly because of its silent quality, becomes a tremendous force that acts on the waves of life in the world of Coins, which can cause a storm and a spiritual uprising and even the opening of the "cups", that is, the human souls.

Between the suits of Cups and Wands there is, as we know, a close connection. The "cups" in the symbolic image of the 3rd Arcanum of Cups form an ascending triangle, corresponding to the spiritual, internal rise of the Initiate; the wands in the image of the 3rd Arcanum of Wands form a descending triangle, corresponding to the initiate's descent into the world.

These two triangles of the 3rd Arcanum of the two suits, together form a hexagram, symbol of the harmony of opposites. In that hexagram, the descending triangle – descending from Spiritual to more dense planes - is represented by the colour white; the ascending triangle, in the opposite colour: black. It is a symbol that refers to the highest planes.

4 OF WANDS

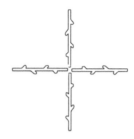

SEEDS GEDULAH AND NETZACH
Traditional title: "Mission".

The image shows four wands forming a cross and pointing to a common centre, without reaching it. The centre symbolises the Unmanifested. The arms of the cross or the four wands represent the four basic types of missiles, through which Initiates of this suit manifest in the world.
Divine Mercy, that is, Sefira Gedulah or Chesed corresponds to this Arcanum and in the Sephirothic Tree, it already belongs to the World of Creation and not to the World of Emanation, like the three preceding Sephiroth.
Wands are essentially a suit of missions that all have the same purpose. There are four types of missions of Wands.

1. The missions of the Initiates who, having reached the highest degree of human evolution, if freed from personal karma and the wheel of incarnations, leave the world and return to their Father's House, making a tear in the karmic net that envelops the world, opening and facilitating the way for those who follow. Such Initiates, in the East, are called "Pratyeka Buddhas". The fact of

whether or not men know of their existence, absolutely does not influence their missions.

2. Initiate missions that voluntarily remain in the world until the end of the Cycle or Manvantara. These missions consist less of activity than influence exerted by the initiate's presence, which is similar to that of catalysts that allow certain chemical processes. These Initiates are Guardians of humanity, are the "Righteous" who, according to the Bible, were searched for and not found before destruction of Sodom and Gomorrah.

3. The missions of the Great Teachers, transmitting and spreading the Divine Influx throughout the world, generally in the form of a new religious teaching with a new aspect of Truth, adapted to the time and human environment. Our present study of the suit of Wands and its degrees deals especially with this type of missions.

4. The disciples' missions, such as those of Saint John, the apostle Paul, of Vivekananda, Yogananda and others. They do not create a new teaching, but they do explain and spread their Master's teaching.
It is easy to see the יהוה quaternary law in these four types of mission. "Iod" corresponds to the most mystical missions, which are purely spiritual and mostly of unknown men, to tear the karmic net of the world (Eagle); the "He" - the most passive missions, are influenced by the presence (Bull); the "Vau", the conscious and creative work of inculcating in people a new aspect of Truth (Man) and "Second He", the realisation, adaptation and introduction into the life of the teacher (or teaching) who was received (Lion).

No type of mission is higher or more important than another. Graduation can exist between Initiates who carry out these missions, but not among their works, because in Wands there is equality of work. The 3rd and

4th types of missions have, in turn, subdivisions, according to the individual characteristics of the Initiate. Thus, number 3 missions can be carried out by several Types of Instructors:

A. An Initiate who has arrived, individually, at the union with the Higher Spiritual Principle and who, on their own teaching and example, opens the way for all those who want to follow them.

B. An Initiate whose highly developed individuality, moves away to leave just one channel, transmitting the Divine Light. The high harmony of individuality and the personality of the Initiate contributes to the quality of that transmission. However, these types of missions of Wands Initiates should not be confused with the transmission of diverse teachings, through people who have a great mental and astral receptivity.

C. An Initiate in charge of a mission who has not, however, finished their own terrestrial evolution. In this case, they will have a greater need to finish it and, therefore, to identify more strongly with the Divine Aspect of the person who receives the opportunity.

Type 4 missions - transmission of teaching of the Master - also have subdivisions:

1. The Preservation of teaching.
2. Propagation and explanation of the teaching.

We also repeat that the value of all missions of Wands are equal, as are the wands of the symbolic image; for all missions, as for Wands, the target is the same.
In the subjective aspect of Wands, that is, the individual ascent of the Initiate, the 4th Arcanum corresponds to Sefira Netzach, Sefira of Victory. However, Wands are not about victory over one's self or the world of the

"non-I", but of renunciation to fight and win in one's own name.

In the preceding grade, the Initiate renounced Higher Peace. In this he resigned any and all his own principles, whether personal or individual, in the struggle with the world's evolution.

The revelation of the mission of Wands makes the Initiate understand that he belongs to the Great Army of Light, the Victorious Egregore of the Higher Cosmic Forces. He becomes one with all those who worked, work and will work for general evolution. Jesus as the Son of Man called these Forces "Father's Will in Heaven"; the disciples personified them in Jesus Himself. The Old Testament Prophets – in Iehova, Adonai or other aspects of the Divine. Ramakrishna - in the Mother of the World.

The awareness of belonging to the Great Egregore of Light not only gives an unshakable esoteric base to each mission of Wands, without which its realisation would be unthinkable, but also influences the initiate's individual ascent, a conditioned ascent nevertheless for the simultaneous descent to the world.

5 OF WANDS

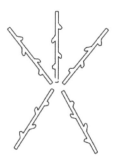

SEPHIROTH GEBURAH AND TIPHARETH
Traditional titles: 'Grand Balance' and "Balance"

The image shows four wands directed from the corners to the centre. The fifth wand points to the same centre but come down from a higher plane.

The four wands represent the four basic types of Wands Initiate missions and the fifth corresponds to the Impulse of the Unmanifested. In the previous Arcanum, this Boost was felt in the Initiate's awareness as Divine Mercy. In this Arcanum it is expressed as Divine Will ("Will of the Father who sent me", John 6:39) or, as in the cases of the disciples' missions, as a reflection of the Divine Will in the Master's will, leading the Initiated Disciple to carry out the mission entrusted to him/her. The infinite Mercy that characterised the experience of the preceding Arcanum, in this one becomes limited, manifesting itself in the world in the form of a determined mission. In other words, Mercy becomes "balanced" by the principle of "legality", that is, by what constitutes the necessary environment and the individual and personal possibilities of Initiation. In Kabbalistic language, the Sefira Gedulah has become as if limited by the Sefira Geburah. It is the "Great

Balance" Path of the Initiate of Wands, who consciously wills the Divine Will. There is no external law that will interfere with this mission.

In Cups, the Theurgic Initiation rose in the great waves of the Ocean of Universal Life to the plane of Infinite Light, filling your "cup" there so that the content could be shared with the world.

In Wands, the rise of the wave can occur until it looks like a separation from the ocean. Every wave that rises in that Ocean is an individuality that rises. Going up always higher, it reaches the Monad. Although the waves that rose the most seem to isolate themselves from the Ocean, they remain attached to it at their bases and each one contains within itself the properties of the entire Ocean. The more the wave - the human being - rises above the general level, the more pronounced their individuality becomes and the greater their ability to express themselves through personality. Most human beings - particles of the Ocean - do not seek to rise above the general level, to form waves; their distance from the Fountain of Light is so great, the Spiritual Principle sunk in the astral and physical envelopes, that they completely identify with their personality.

The mystery of the formation of the personality – a consequence of the separation from the Superior Plane - is one of the most important elements of the 21st Major Arcanum, the Arcanum "Shin". The personality can be formed either "from above" or "from below". The greater the "top" influence, the more the personal aspect is dissolved in it; the more formed "of the lower", it is, of physical and astral matter, in which the higher principles are immersed, the more pronounced will be the personal aspect and the more the human being will be subject to illusions.

The Wands Initiate completely dominates the mystery Shin, that is, has the power to form his personality "from above", to manifest through the Non-Manifested, to concentrate in it the principle of Divine Will, renouncing their own, even when it is totally harmonious.

This "limitation" of yourself, of offering yourself directly to the service of the Divine, takes place, in the subjective ascent of the Wands Initiate, via the passage to the Sefira of Harmony - Tiphareth. There, the Initiate is fully identified with the Divine Will. This results in perfect internal harmony, because harmony is the consequence of balanced synthesis of opposing principles.

The realisation of the missions entrusted by the High, characterises the suit of Wands. The 5th Arcanum of the suit corresponds to concentration and realisation of the Divine Will, giving it, through its mission, an individual hue and a specific direction.

The Cups stage was expressed by a mode of expansion which looked like they are unlimited, a state that corresponds to the oriental formula "Tat twam asi".

In Wands, this expansion becomes limited, taking the form of a well-defined mission, requiring a kind of internal self-determination, corresponding to the formula "This is me".

6 OF WANDS

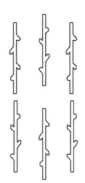

TIPHARETH AND GEBURAH SEPHIROTH
Traditional title: "Rebirth".

The image presents two interlaced triangles, or a hexagram, formed by six wands. In the triangle of the descending type, the ends of the wands are directed towards the lower. It is the active triangle of that symbol. In the ascending triangle, the wands go upwards. This is the passive triangle.
Thus, the symbolism of the triangles is opposite to what is generally accepted. The ascending triangle represents the Divine Influx received by the Initiate; the descendant represents everything he gives to the world, serving it in its mission.
This hexagram is a symbol of high spirituality that characterises Wands Initiates. It represents **ACTIVE PEACE**, that is, the receptivity to the Higher Light and the manifestation of the Unmanifested in the terrestrial world, guarding an inner, complete peace.
"Active peace" is different from the activity practiced in the world, for example, the activity of an Initiate of Coins, in the 10th degree of that suit. "Active peace" consists more in emanation than in movement. It

resembles the action of the sun, that does not AGE, but IS. However, without its light and warmth, there would be no life on Earth.

Wands correspond to an intermediate state between terrestrial life and the Divine plan. In the objective aspect of Wands, that is to say, the 6th grade, Wands correspond to Tiphareth, Sefira of Harmony and Beauty. The highest type of harmony - the internal harmony of Wands – is the synthesis of the passive and active principles that in all other hermetic stages are mutually exclusive.

Tiphareth's Beauty and Harmony are also manifested through service; that of the Initiate in the world, a service in which Divine Mercy harmonises perfectly with understanding the needs and possibilities of the environment in which the Initiate acts. The 6th Arcanum, in the objective aspect of Wands, is the Arcanum of the relationship between the Initiate and the environment.

An Initiate of Wands' descent into a determined environment is the response to the "spiritual thirst" of that environment for that aspect of the Divine Light which the Initiate represents. The "call" comes from below. It is an analogy of the region that is well-known from Eastern wisdom: "When the disciple is ready, the Master appears".

By transmitting his Light, the Wands Initiate contributes to the "rebirth" of the world, leading it in the direction of Reintegration. The traditional Arcanum title expresses this idea. The "rebirth" consists of awareness by the man of his connection with the Higher Principle, in restoring itself of what has been lost, that is, a birth for the eternal.

Wherever an Initiate of Wands passes, the world "is reborn". The biblical symbol of this influence of Wands that make spiritual life reborn is the flowering of Aaron's rod.

The 6th degree of Cups - your Tiphareth - concerned the reciprocal transfer of the content of the "cups" of terrestrial suffering and the Celestial Light. It is necessary to add that, if the 6th Arcanum of Cups the invisible influence of Wands is totally lacking, the "cup" of earthly suffering', instead of raising, could turn into a great burden in the life of the Initiate.

In the subjective aspect, that is, of the ascent, this degree is the Beginning of the Initiate's Reintegration. It is the first creative degree in that direction and corresponds to the Sefira of Severity or Legality, Geburah.

We know on the other hand, however, that Wands are above the laws. Laws do not exist, neither in Wands nor in Wands Initiates, as the laws were established as a consequence of the descent from the plane of Wands to the world.

So, to that degree, one of the highest in the human path, the Sephirothic correspondence, on the contrary, means the total liberation of any Limitation, either by law or by the principle of Severity. It is the superior liberation that, in the words of Jesus, it is accomplished by knowing the Truth.

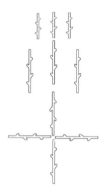

NETZACH AND CHESED
Traditional title: "Great Work"

The image shows seven wands, three of which, with points directed upwards, form a triangle of the ascending type. At the bottom, the remaining four wands, with the points directed towards the centre, form a cross. Above this graphic representation, three smaller Wands, pointed upwards, apparently do not belong to the symbol, but give it an additional meaning. The "Great Work" of Wands - title of this Arcanum – is not, in reality, a work, but the result of the influence of the Initiate upon the environment and its power to manifest the Unmanifested.

As already mentioned, there are four basic types of missions within the initiation of Wands. The 7th degree relates to the way of carrying out missions by Initiates of various individuals, because between the individuality of the Initiate and the type of his mission, there is a close match. In certain cases, this link is so essential that the Initiate's mission seems to be something unique to their individuality.

This is the case when the dominant planet of the Initiate is one of the three symbolised by the triangle in the Arcanum image. This does not mean, however, that the missions of these Initiates are superior to the others, because, we repeat again, in Wands all missions have the same esoteric value. Hierarchical diversity may exist only among Initiates who cross suit at lesser or higher levels.

The triangle represents the Sun, the Moon and Saturn and underlines the special type of Initiates' missions linked to these stars. Their missions have a more abstract character and themselves are less limited to direct transmission of the teaching received from High or from an incarnate Master. "Active peace" manifests itself through them with greater force than through Initiates linked to the four planets symbolised by the four arms of the cross in the Arcanum image. The missions of the latter have a more concrete character. Likewise, it can be said that all the missions in Wands are tinted by the individuality of the Initiate. These can be classified, in general, as follows:

Initiates of the Triangle

1. The Solar type leaves the world and returns to the Father's House, opening the way for others, making it easier for them to rise above illusions. His/her mission resembles the influence of the sun, whose rays pass through layers of the atmosphere, light and heat to Earth.
2. The Lunar type consciously offers not only his/her physical body, but also the psycho-soul and individual system, as a prepared form, so that a Superior Being may use it and manifest in the world through it. This is the case of Spiritual Avatars and mediumship in its highest aspect.
3. The Saturnian type, having crossed all the way for Reintegration, does not pass to Paranirvana but, ignored by the world, it remains, whether in the

physical or etheric body, to give spiritual assistance. Saturn, the most reserved planet of all, dominates in the individuality of Mahatmas or Guardians of humanity, whose simple presence in the world exerts its regenerating influence.

These three planetary types can also perform missions that we call more "concrete" to differentiate them from the first three. We see how it will manifest in the individuality of the Initiate

A Solar-type Initiate will seek to attract followers and spread as much as possible of his/her doctrines, acting not only personally, but also through disciples. He/she will try to synthesise its teaching so it can encompass all aspects of human life.

A Lunar type Initiate will present life from the purely religious point of view, sanctifying the family principle and introducing religious symbolism into everything.

A Saturnian Initiate will emphasise the importance of the mystical principle, of union with the Divine through internal purification, valuing the isolation and the distance from the world. It will perhaps establish mysteries inaccessible to the human masses. His teaching will only be understood by a few.

Initiates of the Cross

1. The Martian type will energetically point out faults or "sins" of individuals and society, inciting people to repentance, to fight against their carnal desires, renounce fleeting earthly pleasures and instead search for heavenly, eternal goods.

2. The Mercurian type will act less by word and preaching than by example and directly influences of their spiritual torment, for miracles and healings. He or she will give proof of the value of internal, spiritual upheaval, demonstrating its power over matter.

3. The Jupiterian type will be a legislator. He or she will seek to influence the great masses, introducing religious

law into the internal life of humanity and in the whole of society, in it the relationships between people.

4. The Venusian type will act on the environment by internal harmony, for the spiritual purity and for the love that emanates, attracting and unifying everyone.

The three smaller Wands at the top of the graphic representation of the Arcanum mainly symbolise the three planets, in addition to the traditional seven, that is, Uranus, Neptune and Hades[8].

The influence of these planets does not act through missions but consists of the special affinity that each Initiate has with the vibrations of one or the other of them. These planets exert their influence worldwide and this is negative for the common man and even for a disciple on the way of Coins, on the philosophical path of Swords and even in Cups, when their level has not yet reached a certain height. Only in Wands, do the vibrations of the three planets become totally positive. Because of this, Initiates of Cups and Wands generally prefer not to talk about these influences, sometimes including them and explaining the vibrations of traditional planets.

Let's just give you a general idea of the influence of these planets.

1. Uranus' expression is via the negation of form. In the world of Coins this leads to anarchy in all fields of life, and the destructive activity in the "not-Me" world. In Swords, scepticism increases, leading to total nihilism. In distorted aspects of Cups it can manifest itself as deceptive mediumship, caused by disorder of the receiving system. In Wands, on the contrary, the vibrations of Uranus allow us to perceive the essence of everything, even when it is totally hidden by some form.

2. Neptune's influence is expressed by the negative attitude about changing anything in your life. In the

---

[8] Probably Pluto, discovered in 1930

world of Coins, this leads to the monotony that ends in boredom, is harmful physically and psychically and results in a tendency to escape. In the most spiritually evolved person it is expressed by longing for something indeterminate. In Wands, when incessant internal transients no longer exist and the fullness of spiritual life is achieved, the Neptunian negativity in the face of changes becomes the will to remain always and Eternally in the present.

3. Hades' influence is expressed by the negative attitude facing the movement. This, in the lower stages, results in passivity, inertia and laziness. In Wands, in an unalterable inner peace.

The positive aspects of these three planets are expressed in the individuality of the Initiates of the superior suits by an imperturbable internal harmony and a "silence of the soul" which isolates them from the world's agitation, despite, and perhaps thanks to, the simultaneous realisation of its terrestrial mission.

In the 7th degree of Wands, the Initiate approaches his passage to Paranirvana or Reintegration. The last three degrees of the suit relate to that passage. It's impossible to transmit with words the experience lived in this stage; in fact, it can only be an attempt at explanation throughout the Wands stage. It is a state of mind that only be sensed by Intuition.

In Coins, Swords and perhaps even Cups, you could talk about the "way". In Wands, it is already a fusion with the Divine, which reaches its fullness in the three last Arcana. At this stage, the Initiate is beyond Good and Evil, as we understand them in our world of illusions. It is a stage where all our terrestrial concepts disappear. The Initiate now knows the reason for the manifestations and their purpose, sees how everything is in its place, because this place was determined in Wands. He/she knows that in the world there are no other laws besides the Divine Will, with which it fully integrates.

The 7th Arcanum of Wands is a kind of sum of the "Great Work "of the Initiate in the world of" the "non-I"; at the same time, this Arcanum corresponds to the final stage of his internal "Great Work", in the path of "I", before the final Reintegration.

In the objective or descent aspect, the 7th degree corresponds to the Sefira of Victory, Netzach. It is the Initiate's final victory about the world of the "non-I", resulting from the great compassion that, permeating his being entirely, led him and made this victory possible.

Now the Initiate performs his union with the Divine Principles of Will and Mercy. These Principles are no longer the external divine, but they became immanent in it; however, Mercy, that is, the active expression of love for the other, cannot exist without the love for God that also became immanent in the Initiate.

It is in this internal state that the Initiate approaches the three last degrees of the realisation of the self with the Divine, through the three "hermetic virtues": Bliss, Purity and Silence, traditional titles of the last three Arcana of Wands. These degrees, in the subjective or ascending sense, correspond to the superior triangle of the Sephirothic system, and each of these last three Arcana constitutes, in itself, a Portal for Reintegration. The choice of the Portal depends on the Initiate himself, of his affinity with the vibrations of one of the three planets symbolised by the three smaller wands in the graphic representation of the Arcanum. So these three wands, in their highest aspect, also symbolise the three Portals or Paths to Reintegration or Paranirvana.

As we will see in the following Arcanum, they have their correspondence in "Sat-Chit-Ananda" of Eastern esotericism and correspond, also, to the types of souls or spiritual states: "Aleph", "Ghimel" and "Lamed", which reflect the primordial differentiation of the Monad and through the realisation of which the Monad returns.

On the objective or descent path, the 7ᵗʰ Arcana concludes the cycle of Missions Arcana. The remaining three Arcana, corresponding to the Sephiroth Hod, Yesod and Malkuth are, one could say, a reflection, in the lower planes, of the three Portals of Paranirvana.

א

ג   ל

Nirvana of Buddha, left wall cave XXVI, Ajanta, India

8 OF WANDS

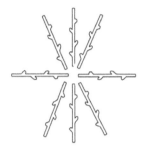

HOD AND BINAH
Traditional title: "Bliss"
Corresponding Planet: Neptune

The Arcanum image features eight wands forming an eight-rayed star. The ends of the wands are directed towards a common, empty centre.

Hod is the Sefira of Peace and Divine Glory. The 8th Arcanum of Wands is that of the Great Peace, which the Initiate lives, because his spirit is in communion with the Divine. This peace is the basic condition of Bliss. The great mystics and saints speak of the Bliss of all religions. According to them, Bliss is inseparable from the experience of the Divine Presence, the Love of God, who fills the soul of the mystic. In Buddhism, Nirvana, in its true sense, is inseparable from Ananda, that is, Bliss. It is interesting to note that in many Buddhist texts, Nirvana is linked to concepts such as: "Happy peace", "Great happiness", Superior Bliss", etc. The complete transition of the soul is often called "Bliss of Liberation".

It can be deduced from all this, that Bliss is one of the manifestations of a very high mystical state. However, most mystical experiences of Bliss, are nothing more than experiences, that is, experiences within time, something that appears and goes, leaving the soul of the mystic in a state of abandonment and, sometimes, of despair, in which the soul is sustained only by the hope of a new approach to the Divine. This state is known to mystics and is called "spiritual dryness".

On the initiatic way, symbolised by the Minor Arcana, it characterises the mystical aspect of the suit of Swords. In Wands, which is not a passing experience of Bliss but of a permanent state of the soul, it denotes a state which precedes and heralds its union with the Absolute. Tradition links the planet Neptune with the 8th degree of Wands. There is no question here, naturally, of "astrological influence", because at the Wands level there are no more astrological influences.

Neptune, in Wands, represents the principle that overcomes time, which cancels the transforming action caused by this factor. In other words, it corresponds to the realisation from the definitive passage beyond the time boundary, to that world in which, according to Revelation, "there will be no more time."

This Arcanum is not, however, about the final destination of humanity in general, but of the Reintegration stage of an isolated soul and its realisation of the state of eternal Bliss.

In the diabetic direction, the 8th degree of Wands corresponds to Sefira Hod and, in the anabatic direction, to Sefira Binah, which, in this suit, is one of the Portals for Reintegration or Paranirvana.

The association of two different Sephiroth is only possible in Wands, where the two directions are simultaneous. Binah forms part of the upper Sephirothic triangle and its association with Sefira Hod has a very special influence on the last three (descending) Arcana of Wands.

The first Arcana are those of the missions and they are related to the initiate's descent and his work in the external world. The last three, which generally also represent the descent to the densest planes, in the suit of Wands, by their association with the upper Triad, become a reflection of these three Archangels of Reintegration. Thus, Sefira Hod or the 8th Arcana, in the objective aspect of Wands, associated with Binah - the 8th the subjective aspect - reflects the principle of Bliss. The more completely and deeply the initiate lives, the more authority and torment will be characteristic of its mission and vice versa: The greater the love and compassion of the Initiate and the more they try to shorten and facilitate the path of Reintegration to others, the greater will be their own Bliss.

We can ask ourselves, which aspect of Sefira Binah constitutes a Portal to Reintegration and what is its link with Bliss.

The Sefira of Divine Reason - Binah - is the passive principle of the Superior Triad and initiates the angelic column of the Sephirothic column that corresponds to the world of "non-I", that is, to everything that can be known, that can be achieved or received from outside; also to what can be felt, even when that feeling is of a very high quality, as for example, Bliss. This is an irrational state, to say the least, but it also includes common human reason, accessible only to Divine Reason, symbolised by Binah.

The symbolic image underlines the irrational quality of Bliss, the traditional title of this Arcanum. We see in this image of an eight-rayed star, which is another form of the octagon, that is, of two interlocking squares.

Two squares traditionally represent the "New Jerusalem" of the Apocalypse, the "New Heaven" and the "New Earth", symbolising the final destination - Reintegration - or the Plan of the Logos for humanity. In the graphical representation of the Arcanum, the centre is empty. It is the Unmanifested, and through this centre all the wands, that is, all the initiate's coins, emerge.

That's all words can express about this Arcanum. Its essence, which is not transmissible, can be reached only by intuition, in a very high spiritual state.

The religious conscience generally considers Bliss like a Divine Grace, a Gift from Above. In an Initiate of Wands it becomes immanent, because the suit of Wands is the transition from the state of fall to the glorious state of man, as, primarily, it was conceived by the Logos-Creator. According to religious esoteric concepts, Bliss is a natural state, both of primordial man, as of the reintegrated one, because this state characterises all Nature which has not fallen.

The "Sat-Chit-Ananda" of the East is another form of presenting the three Portals or Paths for Reintegration, that is, Paranirvana. It corresponds to Western concepts of Existence, Knowledge, Bliss, that is, the Sephiroth Keter, Chokmah and Binah. In the Reintegration presented by the Minor Arcana system, only the order is different:

The first Portal, going upwards – Binah - corresponds to Ananda. Binah or Bliss is the Portal for the type of soul that Western Tradition calls "Ghimel" (from the Hebrew letter "G" in the Divine Name "**AGLA**"). The affinity between this kind of soul and Bliss becomes apparent, if we remember the principles that characterise it: Superior creativity directed inward, the inner happiness that accompanies it and contemplation of some superior aspect of Harmony and Beauty.

9 OF WANDS

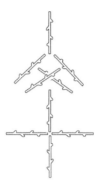

YESOD AND CHOKMAH
Traditional title: "Purity"
Corresponding Planet: Uranus

The Arcanum image features nine wands placed on the card as follows: At the top, three wands aimed at a common point, where nothing is seen, form a triangle of the ascending type. Immediately below, two spiked wands directed upwards, intersect. At the bottom, four wands, the ends of which lead to a common, empty centre, form a cross.

Final reintegration is preceded by a full release, either as an objective manifestation, that is, freedom from karma and the need to reincarnate, albeit subjectively, which corresponds to reaching a state of awareness that does not lead to personality formation. The liberation from karmic laws and the need to incarnate are a natural consequence of the evolution of consciousness, a process closely linked to the relationship with forms and which reaches its final expression in the Wands stage, when crossed at its highest level.

In Coins, a portrait of human ideal, there was an appreciation of form and the search for its most harmonious manifestation possible. In Swords, the form was considered as a factor that creates illusions and was rejected. In Cups, the form was again admitted, but only as a necessary wrapper which enabled the outside world to approach the esoteric essence contained therein. The "cup" formed in the soul of the Initiate to receive the Divine Influx was also a form, though very subtle. This conditional admission of form, in the Cups, achieves a superior expression in the Wands.

Before the eyes of an Initiate of Wands, the form is no more hidden and he/she perceives in everything that existed its intrinsic essence. This results in full liberation from the Initiate of any need of form, even if he/she is capable of finding the right form for themselves and, at the same time, makes them capable of always finding suitable forms for those who still need them. Without this ability, their mission in the world could not be accomplished.

In the nine of Wands, the problem of form is linked, on the one hand, to the Sefira of form, Yesod, and, on the other hand, to the Sefira Chokmah and its corresponding planet, Uranus. This is another aspect of form. So, in the 9th Arcanum of Wands, the form receives dual meaning.

Yesod is related, in the objective sense, to that of descent, with the form of the Initiate's mission, which he values as indispensable for outside work. On the other hand, in the objective sense or ascension, the Sefira Chokmah, one of the Portals for Reintegration, rejects any form, as it is superfluous to the conscience of the Initiate. We will search to understand a little what is the form, from the point of view of the higher degrees of Wands.

Every form is an obscuring factor and also all obscuration is already a form, that is, a limitation or condition. The total liberation of the form corresponds to the **METAPHYSICAL PURITY** that no veil distorts. Purity, the traditional title of this Arcanum, is part of the nature of Wands (as well as Bliss) and corresponds to the second Portal for Reintegration or Paranirvana. Jesus' words "... if you don't become like children, you will in no way enter the Kingdom of Heaven ... " (Matt.18:3), underlines the importance of purity, not just from a moral point of view, but also, as a spontaneous impulse of the child, meaning the absence, in it, of the constraints introduced by reasoning, alien to its nature.

The consequence of Purity is Spiritual Force, whose potential, supplied by the Primordial Source, acts, in turn, not only on the form, but also upon the essence present in every form, thus giving the Initiate of Wands the power over the world.

These two aspects of form in Wands are conditioned mutually. As long as the Initiate is released internally in such a way, both will be able to find suitable forms when needed for others and the most objective will be his choice. And, the better others can perceive a facet of Truth, through the forms under which the Initiate is presented, the more so the Initiate will rise, because the elevation of the spiritual level of the environment around him also raises.

The planet corresponding to the 9th degree of Wands is Uranus. As in the previous Arcanum, the Initiate, in affinity with superior vibrations of Neptune, overcame the time factor, in the Present Arcanum - the 9th - the Initiate, in affinity with the vibrations of Uranus, exceeds the limits of existence through any kind of way, to realise the existence without form.

At Sefira Binah, a passive and therefore receptive pole of the upper triangle of the Sephirothic system, we had the highest aspect in the world of the "non-I", the bliss, characteristic of this degree, corresponded to receptivity, or that is, passive state.

In Sefira Chokmah, the positive pole of the same triangle, the Initiate's consciousness becomes active and actively penetrates through the "Veils of Isis". The Sefira Chokmah corresponds to the "Knower" principle or principle "To know", in its purest aspect, that is, WISDOM, which is different from REASON. The latter is already limited by a way of knowing and by the object or field to be known. Higher, initiatory Wisdom is the consequence of direct penetration into the very essence of everything that exists and this penetration capacity is, in turn, a consequence of the liberation of any limiting or distorting forms.

In the graphic symbol of the nine of Wands, the distribution of elements is the same as in all Archangels of Initiation in other suits. However, in Wands, this representation symbolises the highest level, that is, the limit of Initiation accessible to a human being on Earth. The upper triangle corresponds to the synthesis of the three Paths which lead to Reintegration, their use at the point is Unmanifested, in the Monad and, through this, the union with the soul of the Messiah-Logos. Each path of Wands is, at the same time, a mission and a "sacrifice", resulting from "mercy"; therefore, it is a reflection of the Sacrifice of the Messiah-Logos and a participation in His Work. **IT IS SERVICE**.

Of the three principles of the Eastern Initiation "Sat-Chit-Ananda ", it is "Chit ", the Consciousness and Knowledge at the Wands level, which corresponds to this Arcanum. The same triangle in the Arcanum image also symbolises the three types of souls.

The Portal of the 9th Arcanum of Wands is that of souls of the "Aleph" type. To this generally belong those who seek the Truth: Philosophers, thinkers, scientists and also those who, in the higher degrees of Wands, under the influence of the Infinite (as in the card of the First Major Arcanum), reach the full knowledge of themselves.

The two crossed wands in the centre of the image symbolise the life of the Initiate in the Eternal Present, beyond the limits of time and, simultaneously, the fulfilment of their mission on Earth, realisations that seem to be mutually exclusive.

The four wands that form a cross at the bottom of the image and that, in the Arcana of the Beginning of other suits, symbolise the external realisation, represent here the realisation addressed to the Unmanifested Point, a point within itself, that is, an ACHIEVEMENT beyond any manifestation or external "shape".

The four wands naturally also represent the יהוה law in its aspect of Wands and, equally, the four basic types of missions of this suit. However, everything in Wands has a double aspect and in internal realisation of the 9th Arcanum - the cross - there is also a more external aspect: The spiritual inheritance that the Initiate, both at the 8th and the 9th degree of Wands, leaves on Earth, moves to the Divine World.

This inheritance in the Way of Wisdom, will be the particular form used by the Initiate, in a way that makes understanding of some facet of Unreachable Truth, the essence of which remains Unmanifested, as the centre of the cross in the symbolic image of the Arcanum.

The two aspects of this realisation, the objective and the subjective, as always happens in Wands, are mutually dependent, because the greater the knowledge of the Initiate, the greater the inheritance he leaves on Earth; and the greater your work on Earth, the more it will enrich your Wisdom, from the experience gained.

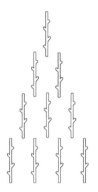

MALKUTH AND KETER
Traditional title: "Silencio";
Corresponding planet: Hades (Pluto)

The Arcanum image shows a pyramid formed by ten wands arranged on four levels that, from top to bottom correspond to one, two, three and four wands respectively. All the ends of the wands are facing up, symbolising the upward movement of all elements, on all planes. However, the 10th Arcanum of Wands is the one that is related to the annulment of the movement. This paradox characterises the nature of the suit where everything seems to be inverted, based on the concepts which are different from those in the world we live in, governed by different laws, belonging to different dimensions if, that is, you can still talk about concepts or dimensions in relation to Wands.
Something considered in the world as destruction, failure or disaster, on the Wands plane can be a definite step forward in a constructive process.

The Arcanum's image seems to synthesise the whole suit: The four basic types of missions, their three Portals or Paths for Reintegration, the two modes - the objective and the subjective - of crossing the suit, as well as the two aspects of each degree and, finally, the union of everything and a fusion with Logos.

The two realisations of Wands - the objective and the subjective - find their conclusion simultaneously in two Sephiroth: The last or tenth, Malkuth, and the first - Keter.

Sefira Malkuth is called "Kingdom". In Wands, it's the reflection of the Divine Kingdom, represented by Keter. During his earthly mission, the Wands Initiate shows the "I" trying to lead men to the Divine Kingdom - Keter. He already lives in Keter's "Kingdom" but to the world he shows the reflection of that "Kingdom" in Malkuth, the only that men can understand. In the subjective aspect of Wands, the more deeply and totally the Initiate reaches the Keter "Kingdom" in their self, the more power there will be in their terrestrial mission and the greater will be the egregore created by them.

The Sefira Keter is called "Radiation" and "Crown". The radiation is that of the Divine Kingdom, symbolised by Keter, and the crown is what awaits those who reach it. The 10th degree of Wands is the third Portal for Reintegration. The traditional title of the Arcanum is "Silence".

How must this "Silence" be understood? It certainly means much more than the absence of any noise, it is defined by that which on the physical plane corresponds to this word. The metaphysical silence is also the absence of more subtle vibrations, belonging to the supra-physical planes, inaccessible to our senses. The "Silence" or "Voice of Silence" of oriental esotericism, already belong to the spiritual plane. It is the "Sat" of the Eastern Initiation, that is, the Real Existence, where there are no more changes, no forms, no limitations.

The Real Existence cannot be described in words. One can only try to express it by saying what it is not; due to the absence of any attribute, time that covers and includes everything that exists.

The planet Hades, whose vibrations in the lower planes manifest themselves by the negative attitude to any movement, in the last Arcanum of Wands corresponds to a positive achievement of the same idea: Overcoming the need for any movement. Each movement has its beginning and its end, its "birth" and its "death", that is, it is subject to modifications and limitations of time and space and therefore is not free of some material aspect. In the previous Arcanum, the Initiate surpassed time, realised the Eternal Gift, went beyond form, by direct contact with the essence: In the 10th Arcanum, they surpass the principle of movement in time and space; break free of the laws that govern biological life and realise the Real Existence, the immortal life of the Spirit. According to Tradition, in the third degree of Wands, the Initiate lives the Divine Life that absorbs individual life. This Portal is particularly close to souls of the "Lamed " type, characterised by the aspiration to unite with Universal Life. The followers of the philosophy of Pantheism and those who perceive the Divine Principle in everything, are in affinity with the Path of the third Portal. These souls are ready to offer what is their own in favour of Real Universal Existence

The fact that there are three Portals does not mean that, to achieve Reintegration the Initiate must pass only through one of the three, but it means that the soul of each Initiate has a greater affinity with one of the Paths or Portals. This affinity is even more pronounced in the lesser degrees, high points of the Path of Reintegration, when the mystical, internal experiences, still have a sporadic character.

As they become a permanent state, the individual principle of the soul is integrated more and more in the unlimited Divine fullness. The realisation of the Internal celestial kingdom would not be complete if experience was lacking of all three Paths or Portals.

The three Paths unite in one, as the Divine Name "**AGLA**" unites the three types of souls. Another Divine Name, "**EMESH**", is formed by the three mother letters of the Hebrew alphabet - Aleph, Shin and Mem – and corresponds to the Triangle of the Archetype. The particularity of this triangle consists of its esoteric meaning, that is, the neutralisation in the direction of two elements by a third party, in the case of a different position from the three elements.

Relating the "Emesh" triangle to the upper triangle of the Sephirotic system, we will have the following correspondences:

Sefira Binah, Arcanum of Bliss - Shin; Sefira Chokmah, Arcanum of Wisdom or self-knowledge - Aleph; Sefira Keter, Arcanum of Immortality, neutralising the other two - Mem.

In the full realisation of the Divine Kingdom itself, these three aspects are inseparable, as there is not one without the others.

PRACTICAL ANNEX TO THE COINS DEGREES

The student's progress on the Coins Path is closely linked to the introduction of a certain discipline in their everyday life and the regular and persevering practice of certain exercises.

Many occult schools, both Western and Eastern, developed, during the centuries of their existence, their own methods, which they often consider as being the best for the student's progress. Naturally this is not so, because, despite the foundations of work being made in all schools, they are a certain way of life. As well as breathing exercises, concentration and meditation, the application of these practices in the life of each student must be in agreement with the objective determined by him, with his physical state, his psychic and mental level and, also, with the particular conditions of his life. What is good for one can be harmful to the other. The student, therefore, must themselves be quite reasonable in adopting some or other practices, whilst refusing those that could harm them. It is important, however, that once the method is chosen, the student continues their practice with perseverance and regularity and doesn't get carried away by ideas that, by changing the method, they would progress more quickly. This would instead result in a sure failure.

The choice of the right type of exercise depends largely on the objective that the student hopes to achieve. For students interested exclusively in the magical aspect and in the development of hidden powers, such as, the development of their personality, there are a great number of special exercises.

The purpose of this course is spiritual progress of the general human being and, therefore, includes the development of the personal principle, but only as a means to the end of general spiritualisation, as presented for us in the chapter of the Coins suit. Therefore, the exercises described here do not exclude those recommended for personality development. Our aim is to help the student so they can reach, by their own efforts, certain internal achievements that will make them able to receive the Influx from Above, when they are ready for it.

By our method, your work as a student consists of:

1. Making your daily life an endless source of opportunities to develop or strengthen certain internal qualities.
2. Practicing the exercises regularly and with individually appropriate perseverance.

Although the volitional development of the chakras and, therefore, of the latent powers, is not a condition "sine qua non" for spiritual progress, the initiatory system of the Minor Arcana uses special exercises to awaken Kundalini. These exercises are dangerous (with the exception of those aimed at developing the heart centre) because, if there is not enough purity and internal preparation, they can cause nervous and psychic disorders. Therefore, they must be done under the supervision of a competent instructor who has their own experience. For this reason, we will limit ourselves here only to general indications.
Other exercises, also dangerous, not from the psychic point of view, but in terms of physical health, are breathing, when done under inadequate conditions and especially if the air is not clean enough. In cases of weakness of the lungs or heart, great precautions must be taken.
Purely mental exercises – from concentration and meditation - do not present any danger. However, especially in the beginning, one should not overdo it or over tax the brain.
We did not mention contemplation because it is not an "exercise". Contemplation is a spiritual state that cannot

be provoked, but that can happen, as a gift from Above, in continuous deep meditation.

Those who aspire to follow the initiation path of Ethical Hermeticism, should never forget that all exercises which aim to develop personality are nothing more than a way, or a preparation, to reach higher spiritual states. This practical annex is primarily intended for those who, having learned the path of Coins in its aspect of Ethical Hermeticism, are firmly determined to follow it; also to those who, having chosen their individual Coins, in one or another spiritual movement, might find in our presentation something new and useful.

GENERAL INDICATIONS FOR THE PSYCHO-PHYSICAL LIFE OF THE STUDENT AND ESSENTIAL BASIC CONDITIONS FOR YOUR PROGRESS

FOOD - Some schools of the occult, especially in the East, are very demanding in this regard. The food consists only of cereals, vegetables and fruits, raw if possible, just like your juices. No one is allowed fat. Due to the large differences in climate and other living conditions, such a severe regime is not always feasible. Furthermore, at the Coins stage, it is not indispensable. However, the following basic, minimum rules can be established both for the student's food and for their way of life.

1. Refrain from eating meat. Meat-eating diets, independent of all the ideological factors of vegetarianism, by ingesting the fluids of dead animals, harms the etheric and astral body.
2. Avoid very spicy food and also tea and coffee, especially strong. It is recommended to replace these drinks by fruit and vegetable juices.
3. From a hidden and not just a physiological point of view, it is important that the food is always very fresh, that it is eaten slowly, well chewed and imagining that, simultaneously, prana or force is also absorbed vital part of food. It is preferable to eat without talking.
4. The amount of food eaten is of paramount importance. The student should always eat with moderation and never fully satisfy hunger. The feeling of being "satisfied" corresponds to excess food. The habit of overloading the stomach is contrary to spiritual elevation and, also, psychic and mental life. It contributes immersion in matter, causes mental laziness, insensitivity and drowsiness. The right food, adequate and reasonable, besides being a purification of the physical organism, facilitates the subtlety of the personality, that is, of the lower tatwas, thus allowing

the penetration of the upper forces. This penetration, in turn, results in a decrease of the need for sleep, food, etc. The two factors - spirituality and physical needs - are, in general, inversely proportional.

5. The use of any narcotic drug is, of course, inadmissible, including smoking cigarettes. This, in addition to its harmful influence, is completely incompatible with respiratory exercises. Tobacco smoking, especially in greater quantity, exerts a numbing action on the vibrations of the ethereal-astral body. The addiction to smoking is sustained by the continuing need to stimulate the brain, which, from a hidden point of view, is unacceptable.

6. Sleep is a natural need and it would be harmful to limit it too much. Similarly, to extend it by laziness or sloth is equally undesirable. The hours of sleep must match the needs of the body. The reduction of this need comes automatically, as the student progresses. It is recommended to begin sleep during the hours before midnight, because of the magnetic changes. It is advisable, also, to sleep with the body lying down along the meridian and get up early. Morning ablutions, if possible with cold water, are considered, especially by E astern schools, as an auxiliary factor in internal work. In the conditions of modern life this corresponds to a shower, preferably cold.

7. Sex life. If complete abstinence is not possible, at least moderation and full conscious control are indispensable. A disorderly, relaxed or depraved sex life is totally incompatible with hidden work. We must not forget that by conserving sexual energy we feed the mental and psychic forces. As progress is made in genuine spiritual growth, it is evident that sexual needs not only diminish, but end up disappearing completely from you.

8. Work. The psychic state in which the work is done is of major importance. A mandatory job, taxing for some vital need and grudgingly executed, weakens and tires physically and psychically. In the case of a work done

willingly, the energy spent is quickly reconstituted. Work done by necessity to earn a living, even if it is monotonous and apparently devoid of the creative element, can be transformed into something edifying, if the person approaches it as something useful to others, as a good personal experience, or, as an opportunity to pay your karma. A job done with goodwill and even with joy, especially when it comes to physical work, acquires a special value and becomes a spiritual growth factor. That's why in many monasteries, work, along with prayer and frugality, is part of everyday discipline. Laziness and physical indolence nourish the lower, negative forces in the human being; work, on the contrary, streamlines and disciplines the physical body. Each student, to the greatest possible extent, should dedicate time daily, even if it is a very short time, to physical work, preferably outdoors, for example, in the garden or in the vegetable garden.

We stress, once again, that the great esoteric value of any work, be it external or internal, is in the fact that it is done with good will and joy.

9. Harmonisation of the four lower tatwas. The degree of development of tatwas in humans, as has already been said, it is the result of your previous work. Therefore, mistakes made by the student will result in the development of the corresponding tatwas. You could even say that this future development is the fundamental reason for the student's entire psycho-physical discipline.

The future degree of development of tatwa Prithivi will relate to everything that, in the student's discipline, says with respect to the physical body. Breathing exercises are related with the Apas tatwa. Pranayama is done, usually in the morning, outdoors or at least beside an open window. Air purity is indispensable. Begin the standing exercise, the body well erected, the arms relaxed along the body. Extend arms forward, tightening the muscles and wrists. Next, slowly bend the arms while simultaneously inhaling the air through both nostrils and imagining that we are absorbing the prana. The end of inspiration must match the arms folded to the maximum. The inspiration must be complete, that is, starting by filling the lower part of the lungs and raising the air up to the upper tips of them, which is a different process of the common human breath in which, generally, only one third of the lungs absorb the retaining rim for a moment the inspired air, imagining that the prana penetrates all the cells of the organism, renewing them. Accompany this mental image with a shudder of the folded arms and tightening fists, as if trying to push the prana into the cells. Expire the air slowly through both nostrils and, at the same time, relax your muscles, dropping your arms slowly. After expiration, start the cycle again. The pranayama should not exceed, at the beginning, five minutes. At the end of the exercise, do a profound inspiration, without participation of the arms and, retaining the air for an instant, expel it through the mouth, through short exhales, as if you were extinguishing the flame of a candle.

For the strengthening of the astral body - tatwa Vayu - there is no better method than to take advantage, if possible, of the experiences that arise in life itself. The student needs to observe his feelings and seek to make them harmonious, because by harmonising them, it strengthens the astral body. Thus, in relation to the environment, the student should always have a friendly attitude, even in relation to the people who are to him, in character and mentality, completely strange. We must try to discover something positive in each being. Until you get to the point that such an attitude becomes natural, the student must practice it, noting and analysing the reason for any critical or hostile feelings within yourself.

To strengthen the mental body - tatwa Tejas - the student needs to try to develop two mental qualities: strict logic and imagination. Thinking logically means giving your decisions a correct basis for action (יהוה

Law), which is very important in the stages of the initiatory path when intuition is not yet sufficiently developed. The student must always act, either logically or intuitively, but never thoughtlessly or illogically.

10. Force of Imagination. The ability to create sharp and stable forms is indispensable for many hidden exercises, even for pranayama. This force of imagination is not the faculty of dreaming or creating, under the impulse of emotions, attractive images, but a function of the disciplined mind, capable of consciously carrying out a task imposed by the will.

Such imaginative strength is none other than a form of concentration, the ability to concentrate the mind on a particular subject (essence of concentration) and the capacity for deep absorption in thinking about a certain abstract subject (essence of meditation), not only develops imaginative power but, in the case of meditation, causes the expansion of consciousness and helps one to acquire the desired qualities. These two capabilities – concentration and meditation - are very necessary throughout the initiatic path. Since the beginning, therefore, the student must dedicate a special attention to them, practicing them daily.

Subjects for concentration and meditation can be chosen by the student himself, according to his individual tendencies

FIRST DEGREE OF COINS

Development of the Principle of Self-Consciousness

The best method to develop the self-consciousness principle and give, in your own life, a predominant role to your true "I", trying to remember it in all the manifestations of life, is to learn to hear your true voice. In addition to the generally stronger voices of all the other small "selves", evaluate each of the last ones and consciously choose between them, either rejecting or taking advantage of them. Make this "I" the constant criterion of your entire activity and, if necessary, give it the role of "awareness" (in the religious sense), which is nothing other than the ethics of the self-conscious principle. The exercises that help the student in this sense are the meditations on the composition of his own being.

The basic subjects for such meditations are:

1. My physical body, with all its functions, demands, etc., is not my real "I", because I can demonstrate mastery over my body, put it under my will or, on the contrary, be primarily conscious of its demands and become a slave to my tastes and fantasies.
2. My feelings and emotions - the astral body – are not my true "I", because they are often also in opposition to my conscious will; equally, I can dominate them or fall under their control.
3. My thoughts are not my true "I", because they can invade me against my conscious will; I can, in other cases, direct them where I want.

By this method comes the understanding that there is "something", a true "I" that can control and rule all these elements.
It is good to illustrate such meditations by the facts of our own life in which the existence of this "something

superior" was manifested clearly. It is useful to repeat these meditations, in variations, until the student is firmly convinced of the reality of their "I".

The first degree of the internal development of the person, the real "I", can manifest itself through two forms: The self-conscious aspect and the ethical aspect. The first manifests itself through the mental; the second, through feelings.

FIRST ASPECT

In order to develop this aspect, the student must always seek to know what is happening and why it is happening. You should also make an effort to observe your thoughts and feelings, arriving later at the point of being able to rule and regulate them. To command the manifestations of the personality, to the extent that this control depends on us, is to rule the lower tatwas. Meditation exercises are of great value if what is achieved by meditation is applied in life. It is very important that there is no gap between the theory and practice of life. If, through meditation, the student really discovers the existence of his true "I", he or she must make it a fact of his or her life. Naturally, to control this "I" over all vital manifestations is much more difficult than might at first appear to a beginner on the path of self-realisation.

If the reality of the "I" has not penetrated enough in the student's heart, he/she will often forget it in daily life. Then, by a freak of will, they will need to come back and be aware of their thoughts, feelings and actions, until that permanent awareness becomes natural in their life. In Western esoteric literature such a state of continuous attention is called an "internal withdrawal state"; in orthodox literature, it is called "mindfulness". Ethical Hermeticism, to teach how to maintain this state, sometimes uses the "priority" method:

"What is the most important moment?"- "The present";
"What is the most important action?" - "The one I'm
doing right now"; "Who is the most important person?"
The one I'm with, at the moment, in direct contact".
All of this underlines the importance of each present
moment and the need to be conscious in any
circumstance of life.
Gurdjieff's teaching, which presents the exclusively
mental aspect, provides many useful indications for
introducing awareness into life, especially habits which
have become almost automatic and are sometimes
called "second nature". These are often harder to control
than thoughts or feelings.

SECOND ASPECT

The second way in which the "I" is manifest is that of
ethical evaluation. This type of manifestation cannot be
developed, but sensitivity can be developed internally to
this aspect of "I" and the best way to do it is to pay close
attention every time we perceive the soft voice of our "I".
Most people notice it only when it has become quite
high and bothers them if, however, they have not
become completely deaf to this internal voice. A sincere
spiritualist is more sensitive to this voice and the
essential condition for its progress is that each problem
of your life, related to ethics, can be solved in harmony
with that voice. If in this field one can speak of
exercises, they might consist only of looking to lead
one's daily life in constant harmony with this higher
criterion.
With the realisation of these two aspects in practical
life, the true human "I" is revealed. These two aspects of
their maintenance are complementary and developing
them is equally indispensable. The deficiency of one,
reduces the value from the other. Thus, the absence of
the ethical aspect results in an exclusively mental

development, and the deficiency of mental awareness - the student is limited to listening and following the inner voice - can lead to a total loss of discernment as to the genuineness of that voice, that is, to undesirable mediumship.

A value given exclusively to mental awareness characterises purely rational schools: Uncontrolled submission. Internal voices are a frequent characteristic among mystical sects. A disciple of the initiatic path, in their internal work, should always keep in mind the possibility of such errors in the search for their Inner Being. Always be aware and in harmony with your true "I", corresponding to the passage of the exoteric state, in which the vast majority of men live, to the esoteric state, indispensable for progress on the initiatic path.

We deal with this first degree more broadly, due to its spiritual importance. In fact, it is the "alpha" of Ethical Hermeticism and the "omega" of Hermetic Philosophy. The path of initiation begins with the revelation of the inner "I" and your search continues, not just through the Coins stage, but also through the higher stages, until the Final Reintegration

SECOND DEGREE OF COINS

Development of internal bipolarity

As we know, the majority of human beings are, by their nature, bipolar, with both the elements "M" and "F" within them. Generally, the characteristics of polarity opposite to the physical sex of the person are less pronounced for their negative aspects. The student's job in the second degree is:

1. Discover the "M" and "F" elements, both positive and negative.
2. Overcome negative characteristics, seeking to replace them with positive polarity opposites.
3. Strengthen existing positive characteristics, especially those of the opposite sex, and seek out non-existent positive characteristics.
4. Practice daily life and creative work on positive aspects of polarities.
5. Underline the "M" and "F" aspects.

First Step

"M" Aspects	"F" Aspects
Psychic Characteristics	
Positive	**Positive**
Courage	Compassion
Decision making capacity	Modesty
Straightforward, direct	Softness
Firmness of character	Prudence
Sincerity	Economy
Magnanimity	Patience
Generosity	Sensitivity and soul
Negative	**Negative**
Hard heartedness	Shyness
Cynicism	Lack of self confidence

Grossness	Insincerity
Impetuosity	Stinginess
Prodigality	Inconstancy
impatience	Inclination to daydreams
Primitive soul	Withdrawal, closed character

Determine the elements "M" and "F" in yourself. We already talked of that in the 2nd Arcanum of Coins. Now, for practical purposes, we give broader explanations.

"M" Aspects	"F" Aspects
Mental Characteristics	
Positive	**Positive**
Logic	Intuitive
Accuracy	Meticulous analysis and deductions
Conciseness, sharpness of expression	Realism and inventive ability in practical life
Capacity for abstract, philosophical thought	Consciousness of the inability to reach the Superior Truths by intellect.
Objective assessment	Concrete mind and the ability to see real life and living beings behind abstract concepts
Retention and honesty in thought	Mental flexibility and quickness of understanding
Negative	**Negative**
Mental insensitivity, inability to perceive	Lack of logic
Making baseless deductions	Contradictions and confusion
Lack of sense of reality	Verbosity and lack of clarity in expression
Mental pride and conviction of being able to achieve everything by the intellect	Incapacity for abstract thinking
Inclination to purely theoretical statements	Subjectivism in thought
Lack of mental flexibility, mental crystalisation and formalism (scholastic)	Mental cunning

It is recommended that the student copy all these characteristics on a sheet of paper and, starting with the positives and negatives of your own sex, carefully analyse each aspect, in relation to themselves.
Analysing them, it is useful to remember the events of your life when one or another of these characteristics appeared more clearly.
It is necessary that the student, when doing this analysis, is completely honest and objective with

themselves and doesn't close their eyes onto weaknesses or hold them up and embellish them. One should examine oneself from the point of view of the true "I". If the student is not sure of any quality, if it is not yet fully expressed, it is better to classify it as non-existent. However, an underestimation is also not ideal. We advise the student to underline, for example, with blue lines the positive characteristics "M" and "F" which he/she considers to have been acquired and stripe with red pencils the negative characteristics that, according to them, are totally outdated. The underlined characteristics and unlined aspects will correspond to your personal composition; to the psycho-mental at the time. In order to observe your progress, it is necessary for the student to have as accurate as possible an image of their condition at the time of internal work.

Second Step

Overcome the negative characteristics of both "M" and "F", replacing them with the opposite polarity. In our presentation, the negative "F" characteristics constitute a counterpart of positive "M", and negative "M", a counterpart positive "F". Therefore, overcoming a negative aspect of "M" or "F" will be expressed as positive development of the opposite polarity. To facilitate this work, we recommend three exercises:

Concentration with self-suggestion, concentration accompanied by psychic breathing and meditation. It is important that concentration or meditation be made based on the acquisition of a positive characteristic and never based on overcoming the negative. By concentrating or meditating on a negative aspect, we unconsciously strengthen the same vibrations.

1. Concentration with self-suggestion begins with choosing a quality (one only) that you want to acquire. Taking a comfortable stance, relaxing the muscles. Breathe deeply and slowly. Focus on the quality chosen (for example, courage) and repeat three times, always in the present and with full conviction "I am brave", as if courage has already been acquired. Say it first out loud, then with a whisper and at last, mentally. This procedure helps to awaken the attention of the soul to the desired quality. The exercise has to be done several times. It's good to do it in the morning, upon waking, and at night, before falling asleep.

2. Concentration accompanied by psychic breathing involves posture and muscle relaxation, as in the previous exercise. Choose a rhythm that is convenient for breathing, for example: 6-3, 6-3 or 8-4, 8-4, according to your pulsations. Create a clear mental image of the quality desired. Such an image can be a personification of that quality taken from real life or mythology, can even be a symbol of it or even its name. It is necessary that the image becomes vibrant with the emanations of the student. Keeping the image stable in mind and breathing in the air, imagine the quality that it represents is absorbed. During air retention, imagine that this quality penetrates and permeates the whole being; during expiration, concentrate on the heart or brain region, according to the quality type. At the time in which the lungs are emptied, the vibrations in the corresponding centre become really active. Repeat the cycle several times, but without getting tired or loosening attention.

3. Meditation. Adopt the same posture and muscle relaxation as in previous exercises. Focus attention upon the desired quality. Meditation itself can be of two basic types:

3.1: Objective meditation on the nature of the quality in question, their typical manifestations, for example, in history, in contemporary life, your expression in art, literature, etc; the various ways in which this quality can manifest itself, about its value in the life of a human being and their influence on the environment. If the person who meditates has literary tendencies, it is good to express your ideas in writing, even if, to do so, the posture needs to be changed. It is useful for the person to repeat this meditation for several days, imagining that it absorbs the desired quality. Objective meditation should always precede subjective meditation. 3.2: For subjective meditation, imagine yourself as possessing the desired quality (always in the present and not in the future). Experiencing, in imagination, as if it were reality, several cases in which the quality in the question manifests itself with strength. This meditation could be called, with reason, "creative concentration"

The two types of meditation can be combined into one exercise only: Objective meditation, passing through naturally to the subjective. It is preferable not to limit the exercise time; that could divert attention and affect creative inspiration, which is the most precious factor of this exercise. Finish the meditation when consciousness itself determines it with an "enough for today".

Exercises to develop internal bipolarity can be done all together or the student can choose one or two, individually, however is personally appropriate. One should never insist on doing or continuing to do exercises that, for one reason or another, don't suit us, either because they cause some disturbance or because they didn't work, after being properly practiced. It is also important that the student works only on one quality at a time and that passes the other one only after achieving a satisfactory result.

It is better to try to develop the qualities first of your own sex, to overcome the defects of the opposite sex and only then pass onto the positive qualities of the opposite sex, overcoming the defects of your own. The positive qualities of the opposite sex are generally more difficult to attain and the experience acquired to obtain those of your own sex makes the task easier. When the student is sure that he/she has developed a new quality, he underlines in his list, at the same time, its negative counterpart.

Third Step

In this stage, the student receives two new tasks:

1. Strengthen all positive aspects, especially those of the opposite polarity. This task, in reality, is a continuation of the previous work. However, in this there are many degrees. The student who initially overcame the most salient negative aspects, obviously cannot perfect the positive counterpart of these aspects simultaneously, as this could take a long time and the main purpose of this part of their training is bipolar harmonisation in general. In the present stage, the student returns to the same aspects with the aim of improving them, with emphasis on strengthening the qualities of the opposite sex. Definitive procurement generally requires great internal effort

2. Acquire the missing qualities. Our list of aspects "M" and "F", positive and negative, is, of course, incomplete, listing only the qualities and defects which are most typical. In the course of his/her work, the student needs to discover the characteristics that are missing from the list, determine their counterpart - positive or negative - and start the internal work upon them. The goal of this step is the total balance between the "M" and "F" elements.

For the realization of the tasks of the third stage, the data provided for the total harmonization can be used.

Fourth Step

Practice in everyday life, as if it were a psycho-mental exercise, the positive aspects of the two polarities or possibly introduce them to creative work. only everyday life can prove whether certain qualities were really acquired.

The student should take advantage of every opportunity to check it out. However, the daily life does not always provide such opportunities and therefore the student himself needs to create them. So, for example, you can dedicate a day to practice some aspect of "M", another day - a positive "F". In that day, in all his activity: at home, in society, in work, in public meetings, in their relations with the environment, in his thoughts and words, he will seek to express the previously chosen quality, surpassing the lowest manifestation of something that is opposite to it.

Such behaviour may look like the performance of a particular role and playing a role is not compatible with pure spirituality. The student must not forget, therefore, that this is just an exercise. In addition, this exercise should be fully in line with ethics, that is, abandoned as soon as the student realises that, in one way or another, it could harm others or that circumstances or ethical sense dictate a different behaviour.

If, on that day, the student decided, for example, to practice patience, a sudden danger may require them to be bold and decisive or, faced with an unhappiness that is someone else's, to be compassionate, etc. If the student has artistic tendencies, these can be very useful for honing a particular quality. Introducing it in some artistic work, expressing it through literature, poetry, music, painting or by some other mode of artistic creativity, he/she focuses on it and starts to vibrate according to what they're looking to express.

Fifth Step

Sublimation of the elements "M" and "F".

The previous task was realisation, harmonisation and application in the daily lives of positive aspects "M" and "F". The task of the 5th stage – sublimation - relates to a higher level: The spiritual life of the human being, his deeper inner experiences. So, the physical courage taken to that level, can become spiritual heroism; compassion can express itself for dedicating his life to impersonal service, etc.
The sublimation of the "M" and "F" aspects cannot be achieved with the help of exercises, it is the result of Previous internal achievements.
In the course of the initiation path all the qualities are indispensable. It is through them that the degree of development of the human being manifests itself, it is deciding, its internal achievements

THIRD DEGREES OF COINS

Creation of the Internal Androgyne

The creation of a harmonious internal androgyne is only possible after harmonisation of all internal binaries. The elements "M" and "F", despite being (in the 2nd degree) developed and perfected, remain separate. The 3rd degree corresponds to your creative union, so the work of the 2nd degree prepares and makes it possible to carry out the 3rd.

Creative union does not mean just an association between the positive elements "M" and "F", but their merger into a harmonious whole, individual and unique, as the internal androgyne retains all personal and individual principles, giving the human being a new value and a new way of expressing life. If it were not so, the realisation of the androgyne would lead human beings to a standardisation that would result in the loss of personality and individuality.

This cannot happen, because, the matter of the human being, from which each androgyne is created, may be similar, but is never identical to that of other beings. Also (and this is especially important) the "birth" of the androgyne occurs through the action of superior principles - of the forces "that create us" - and is also processed in a way that is unique and singular. However, for such a "birth" to become possible, it must be prepared by the previous personal efforts, that is, by what "we create". The following exercises can help to accomplish this degree:

1. Objective meditations on the internal androgyne, its role in human life, its influence on the environment; upon the cases in which it manifests with a special force and, finally, about its participation in the Reintegration process. These meditations, despite having the same basis, must have a different context each time. Such exercises amplify the concept of androgyne in the

consciousness of the student, making them understand better its nature and its purpose.

2. Subjective meditations or exercises of creative imagination on the topic of androgyne. The student must imagine himself as already possessing an androgynous nature and experiencing different life circumstances in which he/she expresses themselves more clearly. These exercises develop, in the student's psyche, the ability to provoke a correct androgynous reaction, when it proves to be necessary in the circumstances of your real life. Such meditations contribute to the effective birth of the internal androgyne.

3. Androgyne practice in everyday life. In high school, the student should practice certain positive aspects of one or other polarity previously chosen; at the 3rd degree they should try to be androgynous in all circumstances of their external life and thoughts. That is, they must not only know how to manifest the qualities "M" and "F", as needed, but joining them together, in a harmonious total; be, for example, at the same time, soft but inflexible, intrepid but prudent, magnanimous but humble.
If any aspect "M" or "F", despite being positive, was to be overdeveloped, it must be consciously attenuated, so that it can form a harmonious balance with its counter-polarity. For example, being too gentle and compassionate can be a hindrance when it is necessary to be demanding and even severe. This "soul surgery", that is, the "amputation" of that which is excessive, can cause internal pain. However, it is indispensable. These are the "labour pains" of the internal androgynous being.

4. The creation of an androgyne in thoughts and creativity can also be helped by similar exercises recommended in high school, but this time in relation to

androgyny and not to the elements "M" or "F". The concept of androgyny can be expressed with greater plenitude in literary creations, where logic can exist together with receptivity and intuition: accuracy in detail along with a thorough and well-founded analysis; the elevation of abstract thinking along with the ability to live practical life.

Practicing all these exercises, the student should not forget that when it does become androgynous it will no longer be necessary to conduct any conscious effort in that direction, because its nature becoming androgynous will not allow you to act in another way.

FOURTH DEGREES OF COINS

Development and Harmonisation of
Hermetic Principles in Yourself

The four hermetic principles are reflected in the ways of
being human, in their composition (static aspect) and in
their activity (dynamic aspect).

Static Aspect

Work on the static aspect of hermetic principles covers,
in turn, work on the four planes of the human being
and the work on the four elements of Nature that
compose it. We will start with the first.

Harmonisation of Planes

This work is divided into four phases:

1. Clear discrimination between planes within the self.
2. Determine the positive and negative aspects present
in the self, from each of the three lower planes.
3. Determination of the dominant plane.
4. Harmonisation and balancing of the three lower
planes.

Let us now study each of these items separately.

1. As we know, man is made up of four planes: The
physical, astral, mental and spiritual. The first three
form the personality. The student who learned how to
be self-conscious must always be able to determine the
origin and the character of the manifestations of their
internal life, noting, for example, when "this is a wish of
my physical body", "this is the manifestation of my
astral vibrations, "this comes from my mental body",
"this is the voice of my true "I".

This practice must be continued until the discernment becomes natural and always clear. It is important that the manifestations of the 4th plane - the spiritual – are not confused with those of other planes, that is, with those of other small "selves".

2. In the 4th Arcanum the positive characteristics were given of the four planes (in their correspondence with the "four hermetic animals "). We add here some negative aspects of the three lower planes in their quarternary manifestation.

On the mental plane: Dispersion of the mind, superficiality, distraction (Eagle); exaggeration of details at the expense of the essence (Bull); lack of logic (Man); pride and intellectual vanity (Lion).
In the astral plane: impetuosity, instability of feelings, changes of mood (Eagle); silly obstinacy (Bull); attachment to certain doctrines (Man); recognition only of its own authority, despotism (Lion).
On the physical plane: inconsistent movement and being hurried (Eagle); too much slowness (Bull); exaggerated asceticism (Man); cult of physical strength and sport as the basis of life or profession (Lion).
The 4th plane - the spiritual - cannot have, of course, negative aspects, but the manifestation of that force, crossing the other three planes (see the cross of the Hierophant), can be corrupted by disharmony existing in them, manifesting, for example, as distortion of the will or creative endeavour. This is the same as if the lower planes, by themselves, are harmonious, the "axis", that is, the spiritual manifestation can also be affected by the lack of balance between them.
The student of this degree, to determine in himself the positive aspects and negative aspects of each plane, should apply the same method already used in high school, in relation to "M" and "F" aspects.

3. Determining their dominant plane will help the student to complete the image of themselves. The dominant plane is often an imbalanced factor as it has developed at the expense of others. This is usually expressed by the predominance given to reason over feelings or, on the contrary, to feelings about reason, making for a unilateral person in both cases. And it is even worse when the physical plane predominates, as it brings the man to the animal state.

The predominance of the spiritual plane does not create any imbalance; quite the contrary, it results in a spiritual personality, which is already an initiatory achievement. When the spiritual plane completely dominates the personality, this suits the state of "sanctity", that is, the Cup stage. The clear determination of the dominant plane is necessary before the student moves to the next job.

4. The work of harmonising the planes is very similar, in methodology, to the work of harmonising "M" and "F" aspects, as was done in the 2nd degree. If the same concentration and meditation exercises are used, as well as the same kind of practice in everyday life, naturally replacing the "M" and "F" aspects of the planes and concentrating or meditating on their positive characteristics. It's useful to visualise, during the exercises, the corresponding "hermetic animal".

When it comes to fortifying one or the other deficient plane, the methods given are used to facilitate future strengthening of the tatwas.

The correspondence between the four tatwas and the three lower planes can be easily established if we include, in the physical plane, the Apas tatwa (connected with the etheric body) with the Prithivi tatwa, as is usually done. In case of insufficient development, either of the astral plane or the mental, the work must observe the strengthening of the weakest plane, up to which they balance.

In the case of pre-dominance of the physical plane (and this is what contributes to the practice of Hatha Yoga exercises, unaccompanied by internal work) the attention given to this plane must be attenuated. There are also opposites in which the physical plane is less developed because of some illness or weakness of the body. This creates, no doubt, certain difficulties in following a training in general or doing certain exercises. In this case, an appropriate individual method must be established. Physical weakness does not make spiritual realisation impossible, but it could make it impossible for the imbalances of the other lower planes.

Work on the four elements

The elements are not just the known ways of the physical plane, that is, air, earth, water and fire, but they are living ethereal-astral entities-formations that constitute the living organism of Nature and its physical body, this is, the Macrocosm.

As already mentioned, the elements correspond to the most dense expression of the tatwas. The elements that manifest in the physical world and, in a more subtle way, in the psychical, when sublimated, belong to the higher planes, finding expression, in the human being, by elevated spiritual states. The possibility of accomplishing such states constitutes the basic purpose of the hidden work on the elements. This work consists of:

1. Learning to know the general positive and negative vibrations of each of the elements.
2. Learning to know these vibrations, in their entirety, or at least in part, within yourself.
3. Determining, in itself, the dominant element.
4. Facilitating the handling of missing or weak elements.
5. Harmonising the manifestations of the four elements.

Let us examine this point by point.

1. In order to be able to know the general vibrations of each element, one can resort to objective meditation on particular characteristics of the physical expression of the element in question. According to the law of analogy, these characteristics have their correspondences in the astral, mental and spiritual planes. In the study of the 4th Arcanum, the negative aspects of the elements were given and also their characteristics corresponding to an elevated initiatic level. Since one should never meditate on negative aspects, and positive expression at the beginning level may be less understandable to the student, we give, below, some positive characteristics of the elements on psycho-mental levels.

AIR - On the physical plane it is characterised by expansion and lightness, especially under the influence of heat. Sublimated, it manifests itself as creative inspiration, especially under the influence of burning thoughts or feelings (heat). It is the principle of lightness (but not of levity) of the mind, the speed of understanding, the speed of reactions and decisions. It is the creative impulse directed outward, into the world of the "non-I" (for example: science, art, exercising an influence on the environment).

EARTH - Symbolises the cold, the concentrate, the opaque, the hard, the firm. Corresponds to the completed, definitive forms, but also the inner, deep and hidden life. It is the element related to esoteric self-analysis, deepening of the self, self-knowledge, discovery of real internal values. It is the ability to hide and protect the inner life of the world's undesirable external influences. At directorial work (for example, of the magician) it corresponds to the ability to establish support points on the physical and astral planes.

WATER - In physical terms, the ability to adapt to any shape, filling it and expanding in the depths, but always preserving its identity, its intrinsic character. It corresponds to important initiatory awareness of the **ONE TRUTH** being able to take more diverse forms and, consequently, the capacity to show the Truth under this multiplicity of forms. It also enables us to share the Truth with someone else, in an appropriate and accessible form when it is necessary. It is the quality that allows you to adapt to any environment, an especially useful quality for a "democratic" type of initiate (see the tenth Arcanum).

FIRE – The element that creates and destroys. In a free state it expands and rises, but in order to emerge and subsist, it needs fuel. In human beings it manifests itself in diverse types of fire, from the most vile, ethereal-astral, like the disseminators of passions and attachments - even the more subtle, like Kundalini, is creative fire that can also destroy - to the Spiritual Fire, which is the Principle itself of Fire and which, in order to burn, needs special conditions.

2. Learn to know the positive and negative vibrations of the elements in yourself. In each human being, the elements exist with greater or lesser force and with their positive and negative characteristics. The student needs to determine, themselves, the strength and characteristics of the elements, using the same method as indicated to determine the "M" and "F" characteristics.

3. Determine the dominant element itself. In each being predominates' one of the elements, in the same way as one of the planets predominates. The dominant planet gives a certain shape to human individuality. The dominant element indicates the essential trends of that individuality. Thus, the element Air will tend towards external creative expansion; the element of Fire brings a tendency to create internally; Terra - to isolate spiritually; Water - to share its internal wealth with the

environment to help it evolve. Determining, however, the dominant element, does not mean that the student should limit themselves to facilitating the harmonious manifestation of only this element. Human development must be multilateral.

4. Facilitate the manifestation of the vibrations of the absent or weak elements. In addition to the harmonious development of the vibrations of its dominant element, the student should seek to facilitate the harmonious handling of the others as well, focusing their attention on each one successively and using the methods employed for the development of the "M" and "F" aspects.

5. Harmonise, in oneself, the manifestations of the four elements, that is, of their elementary content. It has already been said that the superior aspects of the elements cannot be acquired by exercises or practices, as they belong to the spiritual manifestations and are the result of the expansion of general awareness and inner spiritual experiences. However, these superior aspects of the elements exist in the student in a latent state. Therefore, it must facilitate its future management, gradually overcoming all the negative aspects it discovered in itself, fortifying all the corresponding positive aspects, especially of the weakest elements.

Objective meditation allows the student to determine these qualities and realise their importance on the initiation path. Practicing subjective meditation and imagining yourself as possessing the qualities of the elements, highly developed, the student will be able to feel in themselves these vibrations and thus strengthen them. He/she must imagine themselves being able to create how the **sylphs** create; knowing the depths and internal wealth, as **gnomes** know of Earth; knowing how to adapt to everything or in any form, preserving its deep identity, as the water **undines** do; imagine yourself being able to be enveloped by the flames of the purifying fire, identifying with it, like **salamanders**.

To get a good result at work, meditations should be followed, as far as possible, by practice, in daily life, of the qualities of the elements. Especially in the beginning this requires a struggle of will, until the moment when the corresponding vibrations are established and become natural in the student. The awareness, in humans, of positive vibrations of all the elements enriches a lot, not only the personality, but also internal life.

In its dynamic aspect, the four hermetic principles are expressed in the human being as the יהוה law that governs all creative work, be it scientific, artistic, religious, social or other. The second part of the task of the student of this degree is, therefore, to learn to apply this law, both in their objective work, in the world of the "non-I", as in the subjective, internal.

The יהוה law can be explained as follows: **Iod** - the basic idea or purpose of the action; **He** - the material means or others to carry out this action; **Vau** - the way to carry it out; the second **He** - the result I bring.

Each human work, complete and stable, must have those bases, healthy and clean. The same law governs the creation of egregores (in the astral), whether religious, political, social or others. In the case of egregores, Iod corresponds to the idea or the personality of the founder of the school, of the fraternity, society, etc.; He corresponds to human material from that which he has or which constitutes the organization; Vau corresponds to work, in the invisible, that the organisation is doing; the second He corresponds to its expression on the physical plane.

If any work does not bring positive results, if it is not harmonious, if it fails in one way or another, it is because there is something misrepresented or incomplete in the first three factors which consequently affects the room. Failure can also be caused by the imbalance between the component factors (in literature, for example, it will be a work in which the idea predominates, with a lack of artistic sense, or vice versa).

The student must learn to discern well the four elements in every human achievement. He should analyse various human works or institutions, historical egregores, organisations they personally know, etc., seeking to determine the reasons for their development, or failure; ask yourself if the idea that animated or animated the work, existed for a long time or still exists, if it is still current (Iod); if the value of the human material that makes up the work is sufficient for its quantity and quality (He); if your methods were, or are, efficient (Vau). Finally, what were or are the causes of its development or, eventually, of its breakdown: the hostility of the environment, external circumstances or internal disharmony (according to He). In the first case, the egregore may continue to exist in the astral, in the second, it disintegrates.

It is useful for the student to write down their deductions so they will learn to esoterically evaluate various human works. The same law governs internal work and the student must apply it to everything they you doing. That will be the practice in everyday life.

FIFTH DEGREES OF COINS

Unification of Self-Will with Superior Will

In the 1st degree of the initiation path of Coins, the student took knowledge of the existence of their true "I". At the 4th grade, they went deeper into themselves and learned to discern between the four planes of your being. In the 5th grade, one must make an effort to establish the predominance of the spiritual plane. In other words, the real "I" of the student becomes a constant criterion of all projects and of all desires, to evaluate them. The student must accept only that which is in accordance with this superior criterion. Naturally, two questions will arise:

a) How can the personality know this higher will, without it being deformed by interference from any lower plane?
b) How to realise this in practice?

When interference comes from the physical plane, discernment between the two wills does not present difficulties, because only a very undeveloped person could confuse the two sources. But, in relation to feelings and thinking, and the extent to which the personality plane rises, confusion always becomes easier.
Even a person who has high aspirations but does not have enough self-criticism and lacks a deep analysis of the roots of his desires, the involuntary replacement of the higher will by the will coming from the astral or mental body is very frequent.
To avoid this confusion, the safest way is the greatest possible harmonisation of the three planes of the personality, because then there will be no conflicts between the various wills, which then become automatically attuned to the higher will.

Another way to avoid confusing and internal conflicts, while the harmonisation of personality planes is still not carried out, is by always paying a lot of attention to the most tenuous sound of the "inner voice" or "voice of conscience". Try not to act under the influence of the first impulse, but rather try to listen to that "voice" before making any decision involving ethics. Following that "inner voice" automatically monitors personality and harmony of personality, in turn, allows you to hear it better.

In the 5th Arcanum, the problem of free will in human nature was discussed and the inherent conditioning of that freedom to the current personality, as the result of past karma. Thus, the higher will, in order to express itself through the conditioned personality, accepted as "legitimate" certain personal desires and desires that are necessary to the development of that personality.

One of the student's tasks is to objectively assess the content of their personality and determine the degree of "legitimacy" of personal desires, that is, determine which of them are really necessary for the development of the three lower planes.

This analysis should allow the student to always find a way of expressing - in daily life and not just through their aspirations - the Higher Will, in its conditioned form for "legitimate" personal desires. It is very important that this form be realised in the living conditions of the student and not just in theory. Regardless, the student can aspire to a very high ideal, whose realisation is not yet possible, but the way he found to express the will of his "I" must be achievable, we repeat, under the conditions of the present.

The 5th degree is related to the development of the hidden powers. This work, without a competent director, can lead to a disastrous result. We know personally many of these cases. To direct the student remotely, without knowing well their psychic and spiritual state, is not only to take upon themselves the karmic consequences for what may happen, but may also eventually delay the evolution of the student. Because of this, we will not give a description of these exercises, limiting ourselves only to saying that they are based on breathing practice called "great psychic reflection of the Yogis" and in the concentration on certain chakras.

As already said, the heart chakra is the only one whose accelerated development does not present dangers. However, this being the same hidden method that is used for the development of other chakras, we will not provide these indications.

In addition to purely hidden methods, there are also mystical methods to develop the heart chakra. Of them, well known in the mystical orthodox tradition, is the practice of the prayer called the "Jesus Prayer". This, for the spiritual branches higher than those of Kundalini, causes a burning of the heart centre. The method is as follows:

a) Choose a specific short sentence, for example: "Lord Jesus Christ, have mercy on me".

b) Repeat it mentally, concentrating on it and, with that, quickening it.

c) Visualise your heart and inside it "the little hidden cell"(according to the terminology of the authors of the "Philokalia[9]).

d) Repeat the prayer "leading the mind into the heart "(according to the same source), that is, to imagine that the prayer takes place inside that "cell".

e) Practice this prayer as often as possible, when conscience is not concerned with other matters and when nothing distracts her.

If this prayer is practiced for a long time and with a sufficient intensity, the heart begins to "warm up". In

---

[9] Ancient Greek collection of writings by the mystics of the Christian Church Eastern. translated centuries ago and widely spread in the orthodox milieu Russian

the beginning, this occurs only during prayer; later, the heat becomes constant, gradually changing in the burning of the heart. The fire of the heart, being a Spiritual Fire, burns any disharmony. It is the best purifier of the entire astral body. According to the testimony of the great orthodox mystics, in the higher degrees of development of the spiritual (Cup stage), the "Jesus Prayer" continues to be carried inside the heart automatically and uninterrupted.

If the "burning of the heart" is established, the exercises to develop Kundalini become useless, because the "fire of the heart" causing the general spiritualisation of the person, automatically awakens Kundalini and the hidden powers.

SIXTH GRADE OF COINS

Internal Karma and External Androgyny

We know that karma manifests itself internally and externally, positively and negatively and in a pleasant or unpleasant manner. From what has just been said in the study of the previous degree, it can be deduced that the content of the personality, that is, internal karma, is of paramount importance so that the real "I" can express itself.

External karma can be pleasant or unpleasant, but, unlike the internal, it cannot be considered positive or negative, as the value of human beings has never depended on it. In this sense, external karma is the internal consequence, because it is created by the actions, feelings and thoughts of personality. An unpleasant external karma, with the difficulties it entails, should never be considered a punishment, but as a logical consequence of past mistakes. When the soul becomes empowered to accept karma in a positive and esoteric way, the accumulation of your heavy karma is often given to you as an opportunity to accelerate your spiritual evolution.

If heavy karma can be an opportunity for spiritual progress, pleasant karma, in turn, is often a test of internal human value (for example: reaction to wealth and its use, behaviour in the event of celebrity, etc.). If, as we say, external karma, by itself, cannot be considered either positive or negative, the human response to such karma is always positive or negative, that is, esoterically correct or wrong.

A deep objective analysis of your internal karma, whatever it is, it will determine the job the student needs to do itself; external karma will tell you the conditions in which your work should be done during the present incarnation. The clear awareness of this will already be proof of advance on the initiatic path. To perform this work, the student must carefully analyse the essence of his external karma, since, in his life, he became conscious. Special meditations on these subjects will cause the expansion of conscience and will allow, in the future, for the acceptance of karma to be esoterically correct.

For such meditations, rigid norms cannot be established, but a general order can be outlined:

1. Recall the events of your life, their different periods, conditions and main episodes.
2. Determine the pleasant or unpleasant character (often both) of each.
3. Recall your own reaction to conditions or events from the past and determine whether that was esoterically right or wrong and why.
4. Determine the extent to which these external conditions and your own reaction to them influenced your inner life. The duration of these meditations will depend on the extent of the field covered, its depth and intensity. The student needs to recall their reaction to external karma when this reaction was not yet conscious, but impulsive, as that of most people is, to events that are "happy" or "unhappy", the former being considered normal and deserved, the seconds - as unjust and revolting.

The esoteric understanding of your external karma allows the student to perform the basic task of this degree: to assert that in future you will always react correctly to it, during all initiatic paths. This correct reaction can be defined, in general, as a firm attitude towards the involutive temptations (especially pleasant karma) and spiritual firmness in the trials of unpleasant karma. For that, it is necessary to maintain a continuous state of "mind awake" and "sensitive awareness".

Let us move on to the other job which belongs to the same degree: Preparation of the external androgyne. The subject has already been widely treated in the text of the 6th Arcanum. As a practical preparation for the external androgyne, the student can:

a) Meditate on the spiritual androgyne;
b) Create a hidden, natural androgyne.

Meditation on the spiritual androgyne will quicken corresponding vibrations in the student which, if sufficiently intense, will accelerate the encounter with the other half of the same Monad. The text of the meditation will depend on the individuality of the student; you can meditate, for example on your responsibility to your soul mate, because progress in one half makes the other progress. The hidden, natural androgyne, consists of a harmonious union, created by the efforts of two people of the opposite sex, which are or are not halves of the same Monad. The most common form of this type of androgyne is marriage, when very united. Such an androgyne can be an inexhaustible source of improvement for both participants.
The hidden androgyne must be created as "the image and similarity "of the spiritual. For this it is necessary that:

a) The companion is a spiritualist who at least has spiritual tendencies and a similar soul. If you aspire to initiation but have not yet stepped on the Way, it is the best that you get before you get married.
b) The work is done in common, as indicated in the Arcana.
c) The work of this external androgyne is done simultaneously with the work on the internal androgyne (see 3rd degree). '
d) In everything that relates to the formation of a new androgynous persona, there is a total equality of the sexes.

e) If the participants do not know if it is spiritual androgyne, or just the occult, they must always act as if it were the spiritual.

The conscious creation of the hidden, sublimated androgyne is one of the most important practical exercises that life can offer to the disciple.

The 6th Arcana also speaks of the magical call of the soul gem. This requires a special magical preparation and, therefore, we will not give you its description here.

SEVENTH DEGREE OF COINS

Harmonisation of the Internal Planetary Composition and Determination of the Dominant Planet

The job of this degree is to determine the planetary composition, purify all components, fortify the vibrations of the weakly manifested planets, acquire the vibrations of the missing planets; to create in oneself a harmonious planetary synthesis, sublimate it and find the dominant planet, that is, the planetary type of individuality itself. In many ways, this work will be analogous to that which was done in grades two and four and will also be done in consecutive stages.

First of all, the student must correct his planetary composition, with all its positive and negative characteristics. We recommend that you take a list of the positive and negative manifestation effects of each planet and, using of the same system as in degrees two and four, that is, underline and cross out the psychic and mental characteristics and look to "find yourself" within that scheme with the greatest accuracy possible. Usually, in this image of themselves, the student will find the expression of several, but not all, planetary influences, some stronger, others weaker, some positive, others negative. The planetary characteristics visible on the face or body, will naturally not enter as material for work, but can serve as an indication. In order to determine his or her planetary composition, the student needs to know something about each planet, meditate about it and, if possible, understand and "feel" its essence, through the multiplicity of its facets.

Without delving into astrology, however, but to help the student work in this degree, we give some planetary characteristics which manifest in a positive or negative way in humans.

SUN - Positive manifestations: Sociability. Capacity for innate social organisation. Willingness to share support with everyone, deserving or not. Magnanimity. Generosity. Ability to cover all of any problem. At the highest level: willingness to sacrifice for the sake of others, uniting them through that sacrifice. Negative expressions: liking to shine in front of others without any justification for it. Spending, appearing in meetings, public places, attracting eyes. Liking paradoxes and comparisons which have an effect. Proud. Innate self-centredness. Wishing always to be the centre of attention, Love of power. Prodigality. Love of the external environment.

MOON - Positive Manifestations: Ability for thorough analysis (sometimes too much). Maternal and homely qualities, love of home and family. Respect for traditions and nature, hardworking and affectionate. Ability to sacrifice in silence. Many are the negative! Chaotic and contradictory mentality, absence of logical deduction. The important thing about the problem gets lost in superfluous details. Dispersal. Disorder. Negligence. Crystallisation of customs and habits. Clinging to external forms. Moon in Diana (growing) aspect: Tendency to dream, to be romantic, melancholic (over the years, full, turning to Selene). In Hecate's aspect (waning): Tendency to cruelty, sadism and black magic.

MARS - Positive manifestations: Sincerity. Strength of conviction, capable of igniting the environment. Honest and straightforward. Courage. Loyalty to your word and to the work you do. Tenacity to reach the chosen target. Resistance. Negative manifestations: Impetuosity. Impatience. Violence and fanaticism (often caused by the strength of feelings). Lack of frills in desires and passions. Facility to spill blood or incite others to do it. Audacity. Stubbornness. Prone to debauchery, Grossness, Limited and one-sided mind.

MERCURY - Positive manifestations: Mind always alert. It is flexible, ingenious and capable of the most diverse mental operations. Speed of understanding. Subtlety and presence of spirit. Vivacity. Able, in minutes, to reconcile and mediate. Wishing to be in good relations with everyone. Negative Manifestations: Lack of mental honesty. Tendency to prove, for personal advantage, something contrary to truth. Dishonesty. Tendency to take possession of other goods, to be a cheater. Adventurism. Levity. Liking intrigue.

JUPITER - Positive manifestations: Order. Legality. Systematisation. Sense of Justice. Honesty. High concept of dignity and honour. Respect for authority and hierarchy. Respect for tradition, the past and the familial principle. Negative Manifestations. Self-sufficiency, presumption, haughtiness, despotism, irritability. No admission of criticism or other opinions other than your own. Clinging to external forms and ceremonies. Greedy for food. Mental limitation, admitting only recognised authorities and their own.

VENUS. Positive Manifestations: Benevolence and Kindness towards everyone and everything. Modesty, softness, delicacy. Strong aesthetic sense. Ability to present thoughts in beautiful terms, to create mental images. Many are the negative influences! Seeking attractive thoughts and conceptions at the expense of accuracy and depth. Moral relaxation. Trend towards bigamy and Don Juanism. All kinds of sexual addictions, except sadism.

SATURN. Positive Manifestations: Logical mentality and exact. Ability to abstract, philosophical thinking, concentration, meditation and objective self-analysis. Economy. Modesty and simplicity of life. Tendency to solitude and reclusive life. Higher plane - mysticism, wisdom and humility. Negative Manifestations: Tendency to rule only by cold and dry logic, thereby limiting the truth of life and one's own participation in it. Avarice, greed, envy. Tendency to worry about everything. Revenge. inclining to unpleasantness, sadness and coldness. Search for solitude as a result of incompatibility with others and the environment. Bad humour. Contempt.

In the work on the "M" and "F "aspects, in the previous grades, correspondences between the male positive and female negative manifestations were used, and vice versa. In the case of positive and negative planetary characteristics, such clear matches do not exist, however, the following planetary binaries can be established:
Sol-Luna, Mars-Venus and Jupiter-Saturn. These correspond, respectively, to the principles: Expansion-attraction (activity-passivity), "M -"F", and sociability - isolation. Mercury, the intermediary that connects with them all, does not have a counterpart.
Based on these binaries, the negative aspects of Luna can be overcome by the development of positive aspects of the Sun and vice versa. The same can be done in dealing with other planetary binaries. We give a brief outline of these correspondences, also repeating that the work should always consist of focusing on the positive aspects.
The negative aspects of the Moon, such as: Indolence, apathy, laziness, are overcome by strengthening of the positive aspects of the Sun: energy, the ability to be dynamic and creative in the environment, etc.
The negative aspects of the Sun, such as: The expense of excessive and unproductive internal forces to conquer the environment, the desire for success and praise, are overcome by the development of the positive aspects of the Moon, as reasonable economy of its internal forces, capacity to attract the environment owed to certain qualities, indifference to any external glamour, celebrity, etc.

The negative aspects of Venus, such as licentiousness, relaxation of customs, superficial attitude in relation to life, longing for pleasures, can be mitigated via the positive aspects of Mars: Severity in relation to oneself, dedication to an ideal, discipline of customs, rationality in all that is done.

The negative aspects of Mars, such as violence, fanaticism, impatience, rudeness, can be exchanged for the positive aspects of Venus: Softness, balance of mood, affability, delicacy.

The negative aspects of Saturn, such as the contempt for his fellow men, satisfaction with himself, etc, can be exchanged for the positive aspects of Jupiter, such as sympathy and interest towards others, sense of responsibility as part of a whole, desire to introduce order and organisation in the environment, etc.

The negative aspects of Jupiter, such as internally submitting to the purely external forms of the environment and, on the other hand, wanting to impose these forms on others, can be countered with the positive aspects of Saturn, such as conservation of your full independence and protection of your life from the internal influence of the environment.

Mercury's negative manifestations are overcome by the development of the corresponding positive vibrations of all the other planets. So, the calculating inclination and self-interest is overcome by the selfless activity of the Sun; instability in relation to the environment is overcome by the love of the Moon for the home. Its simulation for the frankness and directness of Mars and its lack of honesty in thoughts by Jupiter's justice; its excessive laziness, impertinence and mocking spirit - for the delicacy and friendliness of Venus. Agitation and interest directed to the external is countered by the Saturnian reserve and its concentration on internal values.

On the other hand, the negative vibrations of all other planets can find their positive aspect in the vibrations of Mercury. Thus, the Sun will manifest itself by an expansion that is planned and beneficial, rather than being impulsive and generally useless; the Moon - as life and movement, instead of petrification; Mars – in flexibility and mental elasticity, instead of stiffness and narrowness; Jupiter - as liberality of thinking, rather than formalism and attachment to the foot of the letter; Venus - as new ideas and a practical spirit, instead of naivete and total lack of preparation for life; Saturn - as sociability, instead of isolationism and lack of affability. It is necessary to add that the positive vibrations of Mercury harmonise the differences between all the other planets. Another method to overcome negative vibrations in the self is to work on similar but positive vibrations from the same planet.

Each planet has a characteristic common to all its vibrations. The student's work by this method, consists of transforming, within the limits of this common characteristic of the planet, determined negative vibrations, in others, positive ones. For example, in solar vibrations by transforming prodigality into generosity; in lunar, apathy into calm; in the Martian, violence into energy; in the Mercurial, curiosity into the search for knowledge; in Jupiter, formalism - with respect to tradition: in the Venusian, emotionality into sensitivity; in the Saturnian, avarice – in economy. Having determined its planetary composition, with its positive and negative characteristics, the student can start to harmonise it. For this, we recommend the following exercises:

1. Concentration with self-suggestion. Posture, breathing and exercise processing as in the 2nd and 4th grades. A single planetary quality must be chosen as an objective, and work on it should continue until it is acquired and its firm possession verified in the practice of daily life.
2. Concentration with psychic breathing. The preparation and processing of the exercise is the same as in previous grades. The concept of quality is located

in the cardiac region, if it is of the ethical type in the brain, if it is the mental type.

3. Objective meditation. We repeat again: meditation should be done on the positive aspect, to overcome the corresponding negative. The student meditates on the value of the chosen quality, about its influence on the environment, about the known cases in which it manifested, etc. It is useful that this meditation, as well as subjective, be made in connection with one or another of the above concentrations.

4. Subjective meditation is done as in the previous grades. This meditation should follow the objective. The student's creative imagination must make him the owner of the desired quality, during the time of meditation.

5. Practice in everyday life. This should confirm and strengthen the results achieved in meditation or concentration. However, unlike the practice of qualities "M" and "F", the circumstances to be able to practice planetary qualities should not be created artificially but must be fully natural.

Each action in life has its external aspect and its internal aspect, because before the action manifests itself, there is an internal impulse or reason. An action, however, may not be in accordance with the sincere internal state of the person. The purpose of our training is the realisation of a complete harmony between the external and internal state, that is, the qualities which must become internal. The next stage of the student's work will be the development within his or herself of the positive characteristics, both of the weak planets and those which are not manifest.

This can be done in two ways. The first consists of a work of subsequent impact on each desired planetary quality and the second, in the development of vibrations of receptivity; You are from this or that planet.

The first technique is recommended when there is no negative counterpart of the quality desired by the student. In this case, the work will consist of the continuation of the previous step in which the student overcame a certain defect. If you can, use the same type of exercises.

The second technique: We know that everything in our world vibrates in agreement with one or the other planet and that all planetary vibrations potentially exist in each of us. This allows us to assimilate all planetary qualities. This assimilation can be done by two methods:

a) "Respiration of colour", that is, the concentration on the colour of the given planet.
b) The best possible contact with everything that vibrates with this planet.

The exercise of "breathing in colour" is similar to that of concentration with psychic breathing, with the difference that, instead of focusing on a desired quality, the student focuses on the colour of the planet, whose vibrations they want to assimilate.

Wanting to fortify or create within themselves, for example, Jupiter, the student focuses on the colour blue. If the concentration is done with eyes open, you may have blue objects around you (clothes, ornaments, fabrics, sheets of paper, etc.). If the concentration is done with eyes closed, the colour should be imagined, which is more difficult and requires some prior training. Before starting the exercise itself, that is, the "breath of colour ", the student must learn to "feel "that colour, that is, become sensitive to its vibrations. Therefore, prior meditations on colour in particular are not necessary.

Most people feel an attraction to their planetary colour and an indifference or even dislike for the colours of missing or weak planets in their planetary composition. The student who aspires to create in himself "the synthetic sun" should not feel aversion for any planetary colour and, if there are negative feelings for the colour of the planet whose vibrations you intend to assimilate, you must, before anything else, overcome this aversion, understand the beauty that exists in that colour and make it attractive for you. Otherwise, the exercise may have, for the student, a result opposite to that sought: It will assimilate the negative aspects of the planet. The "breath of colour", accompanied by the creative imagination, unfolds as follows:

During the imagination, the planetary colour or, more exactly, its vibrations, penetrate the organism, together with air and the prana." In retention, vibrations spread throughout the psychophysical body. During expiration, the lungs empty, but the prana, nuanced by the absorbed vibrations, is concentrated in the region of the heart or the brain. During the interruption, the vibrations become active, colouring one's feelings and thoughts with their tonality.

The second method to assimilate the vibrations of a planet consists of trying to be in a narrow and continuous psychophysical contact with everything that vibrates according to this planet, that is, animals (or at least its representations), plants, metals, stones, colour, corresponding incense, etc. As far as possible, physically surround yourself with all this and also imagine that these vibrations fill the place where you live or meditate, trying to feel them. The day of the week dedicated to the planet strengthens its influence, but the exercises, to bring a result, must be frequent and cannot be limited to one day a week. THE planetary time, which plays an important role in magical ceremonies, in this case, would only complicate the schedule.

Like all exercises, these too, to be effective, must be practiced in everyday life. Every day the student should practice the qualities of the planet that rules each particular day and, especially, should try to develop and practice the qualities of the planet that rules its ascending sign, that is, their personality, because the smallest personality defect distorts the manifestation of the individual principle.

The development, in the self, of all positive planetary aspects, that is, the realisation of the "synthetic sun", results in overcoming internal karma.

The unilateral or incomplete planetary development imposes limitations upon the individual principle or the real "I". This one, although it also has a certain planetary character, can express itself fully only on the background of the "synthetic sun".

After having fortified or developed the vibrations which are weak or unmanifest and having raised them to an equal level to the others, the student begins to sublimate the planetary qualities. To underline them is to introduce them and to practice them not only in one's daily, exoteric life, but also in one's internal life and initiatory work. That means cultivating, in one's esoteric life, the dynamic dynamics of the Sun, the intuition of the Moon, the decision and aspiration of Mars, the capabilities in ventures of Mercury, the organisation and order of Jupiter, the warmth from the heart of Venus and the protective spirit of Saturn.

The last step in the work of this degree is to determine its dominant planet or its individuality and facilitate its manifestation. The dominant planet can be found by several means. In the sky chart, if carefully calculated, it "will appear as his "lord", if the student doesn't know astrology, but does have a spiritual Master, he can tell them the type of their individuality. In the absence of these two possibilities, the student will be able to look for it, analysing the character of its approach to religious matters and type of creativity, if it expresses itself in one or the other form.

To find the dominant planet through your attitude in the face of religion, the student needs to meditate deeply about this subject. In the text of the 7th Arcanum are given seven ways of approaching religious matters. Analysing these, students need to find their own way of approach, if not clearly, at least in its essential tendencies. If the student's individuality is not clearly defined through religion, it is possible that its expression through creativity - if any is present - is clearer. To facilitate an eventual search in this direction, we will give some examples which are typical of planetary expression in the field of literature and painting.

In the literature, the solar type will address the basic problems of contemporary society, the lunar type will explore internal life and the feelings of heroes and also Nature, will create lyrical poetry with a melancholic note. The Martian type will use its possibilities to propagate religious, social ideas or policies. The Mercurial type will use the word written in controversy, criticism or in humorous cliques. The Jupiterian type - in moral or educational works and, also, in historical or customs novels. The Venusian type will manifest in soap operas about love and sex. The Saturnian type will create religious, philosophical or mystical works, with profound Psychological depth and the heroes' experiences and actions; also satires about human types.

In painting, the solar type will create sunny landscapes and will use bright colours. The lunar type, on the contrary, will use medium to dark colours, will paint night, autumnal landscapes and also seascapes. The Martian type will create frames containing a very visible idea, it will paint battles. The Mercurian type will combine the play of light and shadow, of colour and form, it will present visual illusions, it will like abstraction, cubism, caricature. The Jupiterian type will choose historical themes and make pictures of the genre. The Venusian type will paint the naked, the living and dead nature, also miniatures. The Saturnian type will create works containing a symbolism, usually of the mystical type. The portrait, per se, does not belong to any particular planet, but the painter's individuality is expressed always in the way of doing it.

The identity of the dominant planet is not enough. It is necessary for the student to become aware of this influence and learn to feel it. The dominant planet already belongs to the spiritual plane, therefore, it cannot be developed or strengthened by exercises, but the student's awareness of being always in internal connection with this planet, facilitates its manifestation. On the other hand, the attunement of religious life and creation of the student with the vibrations of his individual principle, results in greater possibilities of realisation.

Concluding this practical annex to the Coins chapter, we want to add some explanations and observations.

1. The annex does not claim to present all exercises that can be practiced in all grades of personal achievement of the student, nor that these exercises are unique or reserved. Most are practiced by schools and given in the manuals of practical occultism.

2. The reader who wants to achieve only a certain objective, such as, for example, acquiring a quality, doesn't need to practice them all. You can choose the ones that suit your purpose, but whatever your degree and the desired realisation, the practice in everyday life is absolutely essential if you want to achieve a result.

3. In the same way that each religion has its prayers, but each believer has the right to pray in his own way, the Creative insight can also exist in the exercises. The student can combine the elements of several exercises and even create new ones, with the exception of exercises for the development of psychic centres. the creative invention of which could be disastrous. The hidden knowledge and the centuries-old experience created methods for the development of the centres and cannot be replaced by improvisation.

4. It is important to never forget that all exercises and the consequent achievements are, for an aspiring Hermetic initiation, just a means and not the end in itself.

5. It is also necessary to remember that no one exercise will give satisfactory results if, primarily, the internal state of awareness of what has been achieved is not achieved. This state is a "sine qua non" condition of any esoteric work.

6. The practices presented in this annex have been studied for the use of a Coins student. However, they can be followed by each human being who, regardless of any philosophies, traditions, religions, movements or schools, seeks, through purification and internal work to unite with their true Spiritual Being.

Lux Aeterna

Lord Jesus Christ, Son of God, have Mercy on us.

Printed in France by Amazon
Brétigny-sur-Orge, FR

17791635R00157